Build it with Bales

A Step-by-Step Guide to Straw-Bale Construction

Version Two

Matts Myhrman
Out On Bale
1037 E. Linden Street
Tucson, Arizona 85719

and

S. O. MacDonald
InHabitation Services
P.O. Box 58
Gila, New Mexico 88038

Published by Out On Bale

Library of Congress Cataloging-in-Publication Data

Myhrman, M. A.; MacDonald, S. O.
Build it with bales: a step-by-step guide to straw-bale construction

ISBN 0-9642821-1-9 (paperback)

Version 2.0, second printing, December 1997, 4000 copies

Cover and text printed, respectively, with soy-based ink on 100% (20% post-consumer) and 50% (20% post-consumer) recycled paper by West•Press, Tucson, AZ.

Acknowledgments

We are grateful, above all, to our wives, Judy Knox and Nena I. MacDonald. When we procrastinated, they encouraged us gently to continue the work; when we digressed, they facilitated the necessary course corrections; when we despaired of having enough time to finish the task, they reminded us that we had all the time there was and helped us rearrange our priorities. They were, in fact, our valued partners in this endeavor.

Our thanks go to Orien MacDonald, whose steady pen and three-dimensional vision transformed wavering lines, sometimes scrawled on beer-stained napkins, into the visual viscera of this collaboration. Thanks also to Susan Van Auken, Gila neighbor and proofreader extraodinaire.

In this second edition, we despair of listing by name everyone for whose help, and/or contribution to the revival of bale construction, we are grateful. You know who you are, and even if you don't, we're grateful anyway and will see to it that the good *karma* you have earned is duly recorded. In all cases where specific material has been contributed by others, we have tried to remember to acknowledge this in the text and regret any omissions.

Disclaimer

The authors, Out On Bale, InHabitation Services, and the various individuals who have contributed details to this book make no statement, warranty, claim or representation, either expressed or implied, with respect to the construction details or methods described herein. Neither will they assume any liability for damages, losses or injuries that may arise from use of this publication. The details presented here are based on the best information available, but recent experience with the technique is finite and the information will not be appropriate for all conditions and/or climatic regimes. When in doubt, you are advised to consult with experienced people familiar with your local conditions and building codes.

Dedication

We dedicate this book to all the women and men who, without prior knowledge of the technique, were inspired to create human shelter with bales. The rest of us have, at best, only improved a little on their idea.

One thing we do know, that we dare not forget, is that better solutions than ours have at times been made by people with much less information than we have.

... Wendell Berry

Matts' Five Bits

1. Honor your partners. Judy Knox continues to be my valued partner where "our dreams bind our work to our play". Whatever contributions we have made individually to the straw-bale revival reflect that partnership. Steve MacDonald continues to be my valued partner in this book. Wherever it encourages the would-be owner-builder with helpful advice and simple, low-cost, low-tech options, you see his influence. Wherever the design of the book deserves applause, you see his creativity.

2. Help with "the work of the commons". Send a tax-deductible contribution to the "DCAT-Straw-bale Testing and Research Fund" (via a check sent to The Development Center for Appropriate Technology, PO Box 41144, Tucson, AZ 85717). Subscribe to, and share your knowledge, experiences and resources with, The Last Straw, an ad-free journal supporting the international revival of straw-bale construction. Work with others, locally and regionally, to eliminate the institutional barriers to straw-bale construction.

3. Accept some "hard truths" and then "invest in the hope". The "green" building being done today is a very pale green, at best. And, as we are reminded by that lovable, "curmudgeon of cob", Ianto Evans, "All construction involves destruction". This said, we can either sign up for euthanasia or pull up our knickers and help each other do better. "Investing in the hope", trying to form "islands of decency" that can serve as examples for each other, doesn't guarantee success, but "investing in despair" almost certainly guarantees failure.

4. Support the whole "natural building" movement. Let's focus on the important commonalities of purpose, rather than the obvious differences in materials. Straw isn't the only "more sustainable" material out there, nor is it always the best one for a given situation. We need to seek joyful marriages of methodologies, selecting our materials from among those which are quickly renewable (e.g., straw), sustainably harvested (e.g., some bamboo and timber) or literally under our feet (e.g., stone, sand, clay). And even with just straw and earth, we can choose from options that form a continuous spectrum from straw alone, through various mixtures of straw and earth, to earth alone. Regenerative architecture is inclusive.

5. Begin to "Just say enough!". There is "no free lunch" when it comes to building. More importantly, the "lunch" that we in the over-developed world are demanding, will be paid for by our grandchildren. We are "eating" their rightful inheritance. Grafting a "more sustainable" technology like straw-bale construction onto the old paradigms creates only the illusion of change.

The "more is better" design syndrome challenges us to:
- create more space than we need.
- use more materials than necessary.
- assume a level of debt that enslaves us.

The "less is more" paradigm challenges us to:
- create the most functionality in the smallest space that actually serves our needs, rather than our egos.
- use no more materials than necessary.
- choose these materials carefully, minimizing the costs to our health, our pocketbooks and our planet.

To paraphrase a Chinese proverb, "If we do not abandon our present path, we will surely, and tragically, end up where this path leads." A better path can begin here, as I write, and you read, these words. The path is steep, but wide enough for all. Walking together, we can share the burdens and the blessings.

... Matts Myhrman, Tucson

SOM's Seven Bits

1. Keep it small. How much space do you really need? Be honest. Be creative with your space. Pretend you're building storage on a ship. Small is easy to heat...and cool. It's easy to keep clean. It takes up fewer of the Earth's resources and takes up less of its space. You finish the job, at a lower cost, so you can devote yourself to more useful work. If your teenagers need distance, have them build their own outbuilding or addition. They need to learn the skills, anyway.

2. Keep it simple. Control your impulses to make your house a complicated "artsy" statement. Simple, small and rectangular houses are beautiful when made of straw and other natural materials. Let form follow function. Let go of the idea of having a perfectly square, flat and sharp-edged building. Again, spend the time and money you saved by building with straw in other ways – restore the river, help a neighbor, play with the kids.

3. Build it yourself. Trust yourself. You can do it, especially if you build with straw. And especially if you follow rules 1 and 2. Read building books and magazines. Ask your builder friends questions. Build it on paper and as a model first. Track the details. Use your common sense. Be creative with your mistakes. Don't be intimidated by the "experts". Get all the stuff together and host a straw-bale "barn raising".

4. Stay out of debt. Pay as you go. Assemble the parts as you have the money...and time. Make your barn raising a "potluck."

5. Use local materials. Use more rock and adobe, less concrete. Use locally-milled lumber and poles. Your neighbor needs the work and you need to know firsthand what demands you're asking of the forests and fields.

6. Be energy conscious. Build to maximize passive heating/cooling strategies. Superinsulate your ceiling. Disconnect from the electric power grid. Use a solar pump. Build a composting toilet. Raise a garden. Throw out the television.

7. Make yourself a home. Don't just build yourself a house, make yourself a home. Stay where you are, if you can. Learn to be at home. Do no harm.

... Stephen O. MacDonald, Gila

Matts Myhrman lives with his life-and-business partner, Judy Knox (who helped proofread this guide), just south of The Little Taj in Tucson, Arizona. He is an extinguished geo-hydrologist who plans to spend his retirement promoting straw-bale and other alternative building methods (so what's new?).

Photo credit Nena MacDonald

Stephen O. MacDonald inhabits the Gila River Valley with wife Nena, along with a host of good neighbors—human and otherwise. Steve, with his love for rats, bats, and other wild creatures, tries to return each summer to his former home in Alaska as a research associate with the University of Alaska Museum.

Contents

Introduction

Why We Wrote the 1st Edition of This Guide

At some point in the yeasty revival of an "alternative" building method, the initial rapid pace of growth and change begins to slow down a little. Experimentation and learning will continue, but there now exists a body of knowledge that has already been validated by experience. Desktop publishing provides an economic way to start sharing such knowledge in printed form. It also allows future revision and expansion on a timely basis. So until someone chooses to publish the official, hard-backed, "complete and unabridged" bible of straw-bale construction, here's grist for the mill from two battle-scarred practitioners.

Why a 2nd Edition, Why Now?

In the three years since the birth of the 1st edition (a.k.a. *Version 1.0*), interest in, and use of, bales for building has increased beyond our wildest dreams. There are now bale structures in nearly all of the 50 states of the USA and in many other countries as well. The homes run the gamut from examples of "enough" (usually owner-built) to classic examples of "eco-over-consumption" (usually professionally designed and built to the client's specifications). The commercial buildings include workshops/studios (for potters, painters, woodworkers, blacksmiths), a counseling center, wineries, churches and bed-and-breakfasts.

From that great teacher, "experience", a great deal has been learned about using bales to make good buildings. Unfortunately, some of the lessons have come from the "school of hard knocks" (e.g., the flammability of loose straw, and even loose bales, under windy conditions). On a more positive note, creative practitioners around the world have come up with new options, new techniques, and new tools, many of which have been shared via *The Last Straw*—the journal of the straw-bale revival. We've been sticking notes about these things in manila folders until they wouldn't hold any more. What clearer message from the universe can two reluctant writers get? So, until the folders get full again, here's our revised, expanded and (hopefully) improved *Version 2.0*.

What's the Same and What's Different

Readers familiar with the first edition will quickly see that **many things are the same**. We haven't tampered with the basic organization of the information, since it reportedly worked well for our readers. We also continue here to devote more pages to the *Loadbearing Option* than to the *Non-Loadbearing Option*. We don't intend this to be a book that will provide detailed information on all the various ways in which you can use materials, other than bales, to support the weight of the roof. There are already good resources out there for this, and we refer you to some of them.

Since many things are basically the same for both approaches (e.g., stacking, pinning, surfacing), we ask that readers who have chosen the non-loadbearing option study first the material about the loadbearing option. Having learned about building straw-bale walls, they can then turn to the material on the non-loadbearing option for information about how to create a bale-superinsulated framework.

This said, let's look at **what's different** about this second edition:

• **Reductions**. We have reduced the coverage of some topics which can now be accessed elsewhere (e.g., testing and building codes).

• **Deletions**. Because each year's Summer Issue of *The Last Straw* will feature an updated, comprehensive directory of straw-bale resources of all kinds, we have eliminated the appendices that provided only a modest amount of such information in the first edition. "How-to" options that have fallen out of general use have also been eliminated.

• **Expansions**. Using all this newly available space, and more, we have added to the coverage of many topics. *Step 7, Surfacing the Walls* has undergone major expansion.

• **Additions**. We have added one totally new item that we hope will be of great use to our readers—an *Index*.

How This Guide is Organized

We've divided the main body of the guide into two parts: *Part One* deals with the things you may want to know, think about or do before you build; *Part Two* takes you through the building process. For both the *Loadbearing Option* and the *Non-Loadbearing Option*, we focus on the "model" structure depicted in the

overview drawing placed at the beginning of these two sections.

Each *Step*, in both sections, starts off with our attempt to describe succinctly the generalized *Challenge* the builder faces at this stage in the process. This approach reflects our vision of this guide as a resource for the decision-making process you will step through on the way from your first fantasies to the first (of many) housewarming parties. At each major step in this process, the decision-making context will be unique. The *Challenge* facing you will have many possible solutions. Your shaping of the right solution for your unique situation will reflect many variables which only you can quantify or assess. Consider the following:

• your financial situation;
• your timetable;
• regional and micro-climatic factors and other physical characteristics of your building site;
• your own availability as a worker and your skill level in various areas;
• the availability of additional volunteer or paid labor at various skill levels;
• the depth of your concerns about the sustainability, regional availability, healthiness and life-cycle costs of various materials;
• the degree to which you want to use your time and labor to "buy" materials that have little or no monetary cost;
• your personal comfort level for cost-cutting innovation/greater risk as opposed to typical overbuilding/greater security;
• and, your aesthetic preferences, your willingness to pay for them, and their planetary costs.

The uniqueness of this combination of site, builder and building design suggests to us that a "cookbook" approach will not best serve you, our readers. There is no one "right" way to build a straw-bale structure or even to solve the problems to be faced at any given stage in the process. However, equipped with:

• a modicum of common sense;

• a clear understanding of each *Challenge* and of the unique properties of these big, fuzzy bricks as a building material;

• and, an array of options successfully used by earlier builders.

We can all hope to shape solutions that are uniquely "right" for us. As Amy Klippenstein and Paul Lacinski (1996) put it: "There are only individual solutions, arrived at by the thoughtful synthesis of regional identity and personal need into buildings that work for the inhabitants and the places where we chose to build them."

Each *Challenge* is followed by an arguably chronological *Walk-Through* of the mini-steps that we envision taking you through this stage in the construction of the "model" building. These are highlighted using the symbol "♣". Interspersed with these "model"-related mini-steps are chunks of predominantly non-visual, generic information relevant to the decision-making required during this *Step*.

Following the *Walk-Through* you will find textual and graphic coverage of an array of options that have been used successfully by straw-bale builders. Please note that our drawings are not necessarily "to scale", are not presented as backed by any "engineering", and are intended as general depiction of options, rather than "working drawings".

Throughout the guide we have tried to focus on those aspects of plan development and construction made unique by the decision to "build it with bales". Rather than repeating detailed information from other helpful sources, we provide literature citations (author, year of publication) for them. Complete citations are provided in the *Literature Cited* section near the end of the guide.

As you read this book you will encounter many places in which we refer you to an article in a back issue of *The Last Straw*. We realize that for some readers this may result in frustration, but we could see only three options:

1) lengthy, illustrated coverage that could stand alone;

2) a brief description or small drawing, accompanied by a citation;

3) or, no coverage of the matter at all.

Choosing 1) would have made the book too long and unconscionably expensive, while choosing 3) would have left it unacceptably incomplete. So we chose 2) as the least of the evils, hoping that you will be able to do one of the following:

• Borrow selected issues from a friend;

• find them at your local library or have your library get them through interlibrary loan;

• or, buy the appropriate back issues.

Ways to Use this Book

It's not heavy enough to be a good doorstop and the movie version isn't out yet, so you might as well read it. If you're new to straw-bale, we recommend that you start at the beginning and slog straight on through. Just remember to breathe occasionally and stop to volunteer for wall-raisings. If you already have experience building with bales, you may choose to use the *Table of Contents* and/or the *Index* to go directly to what most interests you, buffet-style.

Roots

The saga of building human habitation with rectangular bales of hay or straw begins with the availability of mechanical devices to produce them. Hand-operated hay presses were patented in the United States before 1850, and by 1872 one could purchase a stationary, horse-powered baler. By about 1884, steam-powered balers were available, but the earlier horse-powered versions also continued to be used in the Great Plains at least through the 1920's.

We will probably never know any details of the first "permanent" bale-walled building used to shelter human beings. It seems likely, however, that it's creator was a homesteader, recently arrived on the treeless grasslands of the Great Plains and in desperate need of quick, inexpensive protection from a harsh climate. Although homesteading came to the Sandhills of Nebraska later than other parts of the Plains, it is here that we find the first, documented use of bales in a "permanent" building. The one-room, hay-bale schoolhouse, built in 1896 or 1897 near Scott's Bluff, survived only a few years before being eaten by cows.

The illustration, shown right (adapted from Welsch 1973), provides a visual description of the technique apparently used in many of the early buildings. Although Welsch's diagram doesn't show the ties, we know that bales were used both "flat" and "on edge" (see diagram top right) and that in some cases the bales were laid up with a lime/sand mortar. Of particular importance is the lack of any vertical posts to carry the weight of the light (generally hipped) roof.

Use of the technique in Nebraska, most widespread from about 1915 to 1930, appears to have ended by 1940. Of the approximately

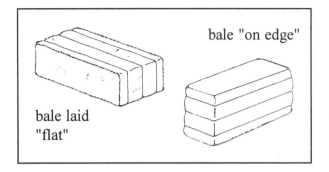

seventy structures from this period documented by Welsch (1970), thirteen were known to still exist in 1993 and all but one of these (the oldest, from 1903) were still being lived in or used for storage.

The demise of the others can almost certainly be attributed to lack of maintenance resulting from abandonment. Once water begins to get through the roof and into the walls, a protracted death is inevitable.

Early Hay-Bale Building Techniques
(adapted from an illustration in Welsch, 1973)

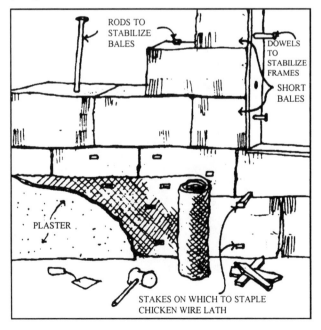

Photo by Matts Myhrman

The Burke House, near Alliance, Nebraska, built in 1903.

Photo by Matts Myhrman

Dr. Burritt's bale-insulated mansion, Huntsville, Alabama, finished in 1938.

... and Revival

After its abandonment in Nebraska by 1940, the idea of bale construction wandered in search of folks motivated to build inexpensive, energy-efficient shelter. Rather than dying out, the method kept popping up in new locations as modern pioneers learned of it or reinvented it.

Welsch's 1973 article in *Shelter* introduced the concept to a readership actively seeking alternatives. Another very important article, which appeared in the mainstream magazine *Fine Homebuilding* (Strang, 1983), described a small, post-and-beam studio designed and built by California architect Jon Hammond. In 1987, New Mexicans Steve and Nena MacDonald, two of the many individuals inspired by Strang's article, finally overcame their fears and built themselves a wonderful home that soon came to the attention of Matts Myhrman and Judy Knox.

Inspired by Steve's and Nena's home and philosophy, and building on the work of straw-bale pioneer David Bainbridge, Matts and Judy researched the historic hay- and straw-bale homes in Nebraska. Encouraged by what they learned, they went on to set up *Out On Bale*, a straw-bale-construction education and resource center and begin publication of *The Last Straw*, the journal of straw-bale construction. Meanwhile, Steve continued to help/teach others to build with bales and, with his son, Orien, developed the straw-bale construction primer that the first edition of this guide expanded on.

Meanwhile, the technique was being used almost exclusively in rural areas, where people could build "without benefit of codes". It became clear that in order for the technique to be legal in more populated areas, structural testing related to wind and seismic forces would have to be carried out. And so, for the first time, the concept of the "straw-bale commons" drew together a group of individuals willing to invest their money, time and energy for the benefit of the whole revival. This testing, begun in Tucson, AZ, has since been continued in other states (especially New Mexico) and other countries (see *The Last Straw*, Issue 15, page 19 for a list of reports on research and testing). Based on the Tucson testing, author Matts and David Eisenberg, began the arduous process of winning code approval for non-loadbearing <u>and</u> loadbearing straw-bale construction in Tucson and Pima County, AZ. Nearly two years later, in January of 1996, after seven drafts and intense negotiating, the document was approved. By that time, it was already being used to develop guidelines for jurisdictions in California, Nevada, and Texas (for details, see *The Last Straw*, Issue No. 15, page 16). Guidelines for the non-loadbearing approach only, have been approved in New Mexico (for a copy of either code, call *Out On Bale—By Mail* at (602) 624-1673, or *The Development Center for Appropriate Technology* at (520) 624-6628. The code phenomenon is slowly developing momentum, as new testing provides additional support for approval.

At the same time, as interest in the technique continued to grow, the need for written and videographic resources became acute. In 1994, two substantive stand-alone books became available (i.e., the first edition of this opus and *The Straw Bale House*). These have been complemented, for the "print-challenged" among us, by several pioneering videos produced by Catherine Wanek & Friends and by Steve Kemble & Carol Escott.

The unique combination of environmental,

socioeconomic and natural resource issues facing our species as we approach the 21st century challenge us to expand the choices that will lead us toward more sustainable systems. We see this legacy of bale construction, passed on to us by our homesteading ancestors, as one such choice, a beautiful baby that got thrown out with the bath water, but managed not to go down the drain.

Virginia Carabelli's straw-bale home under construction near Santa Fe, New Mexico, spring 1991.

Photo by Matts Myhrman

Photo by David Eisenberg

Virginia Carabelli's straw-bale home after completion, autumn 1991.

Questions and Answers

Q. What do North American builders mean by the word "bale"?
A. They usually mean a variously-sized, rectangular bundle of plant stems, held together by two or three ties of wire or baling twine and weighing from about 35 to 95 pounds [16 to 43 kg]. Such bales generally consist of "straw", the dry, dead stems that remain after the removal of seed from harvested cereal grains. This is an annually renewable, little-valued byproduct of cereal grain production and great quantities are available for baling in many parts of the world.

Q. If straw-bale construction becomes very widely used (the authors' dream), won't it become difficult to find bales?
A. Basing our answer on the amount of baleable straw that is available every year in North America, we can answer with a resounding "No!". Assuming that about 140 million tons [about 127 metric tonnes] are available to bale each year and that we only use 25% of this, (the remainder being incorporated back into the soil for the uncertain benefits this might provide), we are left with a mere 35 million tons [31.75 million tonnes](Wilson 1995b). If we assume that all of this tonnage is made into 85 pound [about 38.6 kg], three-tie bales, we would have 823,529,411 bales at our disposal. Using the chart on page 20, we can determine that it will take about 260 three-tie bales to build the six-course high walls (about 8 feet, or 2.44 meters) of a modestly rectangular house having an interior square footage of 1500 square feet [about 139 square meters].

A simple division yields a stunning result. Using only one-quarter of the straw available each year in North America, we could build slightly more than 3 million such houses. Now that's a dream that even your authors find hard to assimilate.

Q. What would constitute the ideal "construction grade" bale?
A. It would be very dry, free from seeds, well-compacted, consistent in size and shape, and have a length that is twice the width. More on this on page 15.

Q. Will you always find such bales readily available anywhere?
A. Unfortunately not, but there is usually something grown within reasonable trucking distance that can be baled for building. However, in some areas the only bales available are the big, round ones. We trust that as demand develops globally for "construction grade" bales, entrepreneuring farmers will gladly meet the demand. Sources for bales can often be provided by agricultural extension agents, grain growers associations, tack and feed stores, zoos and race tracks. If you can work directly with a farmer, you have a better chance of getting bales that approach the ideal.

Q. Can a bale be too well-compacted?
A. From a strictly structural standpoint, the answer is no. However, as the bale density increases beyond a certain point, the insulation value per unit of thickness will begin to decrease. This results from a decrease in the amount of trapped air in the

bale, it being this trapped air that actually provides most of the insulating value of baled straw. Another disadvantage of very dense bales is that they become more difficult to penetrate with pins, stakes, dowels, etc., and they become harder to lift and stack (especially noticeable with the larger three-tie bales). Based on the above, the ideal bale for wall-building would have a calculated density no greater than about 8.5 pounds per cubic foot [about 137 kg per cubic meter]. For ceiling insulation, consider using the typically lighter two-tie bales. They will add less to the compressive load on the walls, and will provide more insulation value per unit of thickness.

Q. What are loadbearing versus non-loadbearing straw-bale walls?
A. Loadbearing walls carry a share of the roof loads, both "dead" (i.e., roof/ceiling materials) and "live" (e.g., snow, humans). Non-loadbearing walls, either because of the roof shape or the presence of a complementary framework, carry none of the roof weight. More on this later.

Q. Is straw-bale construction, particularly when done with loadbearing walls (a.k.a. Nebraska-style), inherently less costly?
A. A custom-designed straw-bale house built in mainstream fashion, by a contractor using only paid labor, cannot cost significantly less than a frame or masonry house providing the same interior space. From the standpoint of a cold-blooded, profit-margin-driven cost estimator, this is just an exterior wall system. The cost (labor and materials) attributable to the exterior walls of modest homes generally accounts for only fifteen to twenty percent of the total project cost. Using straw bales to replace insulation,

and wood, metal, or masonry, can only affect this already small piece of the pie. The cost increases due to wider foundations and greater required roof area will offset some or all of these savings.

Real savings begin when the eventual owner and friends provide the labor for the wall-raising, wall-surfacing and for interior finishing. Additional savings can result from the use of recycled materials and those that cost little more than the owner's time (*e.g.*, salvaged lumber, locally available stone and earth). Further savings result wherever the owner-builder can substitute his/her own labor for paid labor or reduce costs by assisting a paid tradesperson.

The Straw Bale Workbook (Bolles 1996) contains a wealth of useful information, especially for California builders. In *Chapter 5*, the author provides a quantitative analysis comparing the 30-year and 100-year life-cycle costs for a conventionally built home with three straw-bale homes built with varying levels of both owner-contributed labor and bank financing. Suffice it to say that the bale buildings all had significantly lower costs, for both the 30- and 100-year cycles.

But even if a straw-bale house does end up costing as much as its counterpart, we believe it will still be a better house—quieter, more energy-efficient, more joyful to live in and, if designed with this in mind, less costly to the planet's ecological systems. For a brief look at how straw-bale construction rates ecologically, see Edminster (1997). For a 120-page report entitled *Investigation of Environmental Impacts: Straw-bale Construction* contact Ann Edminster at 115 Angelita Ave., Pacifica, CA 94004 or by e-mail at <74200.746@compuserv.com>.

Q. Okay, but what about termites?

A. A house built of baled straw is at far less risk than a wood-frame building, at least in North America and Canada, since virtually all the termites found there are specifically evolved to tunnel into and eat solid wood. Some builders do use some type of chemical or biological strategy, however, if only to protect wooden door and window frames and furniture. In areas where termites are a severe problem, or where a species of grass-eating termite is found, a metal termite shield should also be included in the foundation design. This is especially true when perimeter insulation is used, since termites use the insulation as an invisible corridor through which to reach the walls.

Q. All right, but what about spontaneous combustion in a baled straw wall?

A. Spontaneous combustion can occur in large, tight stacks of **hay**, baled while still too green and wet. However, we have been able to document no case of this occurring with straw bales stacked in a wall.

Q. Yeah, but what about fire?

A. As long as the bales are covered with plaster, a bale building will be extremely fire-resistant. Exposed bales and loose straw will burn under certain circumstances, however, so **caution is advised** (see page 18).

Q. Then what about vermin (i.e., rodents and insects)? Do the bales need any special chemical treatment to protect against them?

A. As in a frame structure, the secret lies in denying unwanted critters a way to get in and out of your walls. Build so as to isolate the bales (including the tops of the walls) and then regularly check and repair the exterior and interior wall surfacing. A few modern builders have used bales with lime incorporated into them or have dipped or sprayed the bales using a lime slurry or borate solution. Such measures may provide an extra level of insurance if maintenance of the wall surfacings is poor.

Q. Do I need to protect my stacked bales and/or exposed walls from musk oxen, llamas, slow elk (a.k.a. cows), or other roaming ruminants?

A. Yes, you do. Only if very hungry will they actually eat the straw, but the aroma of the straw seems to suggest to them the presence of something tasty just a little further into the bale. They'll use their horns and/or teeth to remove straw and can do major damage, especially at corners. If such critters have access to your building site, you would be well advised to fence it.

Q. Is straw-bale construction suitable for all climates?

A. The only serious enemy of straw is prolonged exposure to water in liquid form, since with sufficient moisture present, fungi produce enzymes which break down the cellulose in stems. High humidity, by itself, does not appear to be a problem, but few historic examples exist from areas characterized by consistently high relative humidity. However, one accessible example is the Burritt Mansion, part of a city park in Huntsville, Alabama. Built in 1930 in a climate characterized by high humidity and a 50 inch [1.26 m] average annual rainfall, it seems to be doing very well. Walls exposed to high humidity from within or without could experience condensation within the walls during periods of extremely cold temperatures. In such situations, moisture barriers (in reality, barriers to the movement of air and water vapor) are sometimes used. They are most typically placed on, or within, the inner surface of the exterior walls, the ceiling, and the floors. For guidance on building in cold or cold/wet climates, see CMHC (1994), ACHP (1995), and Lstiburek (1997).

Airtight designs for cold climates often require the use of an air exchanger to maintain healthy indoor air quality and humidity levels. The use of exhaust fans to remove humid air from kitchens and bathrooms is typical.

High rainfall can be dealt with by proper design and detailing (e.g., adequate roof overhangs, flashing at window and door openings) and regular maintenance of the roof and wall surfaces. Since thick bale walls are highly insulative, the ideal climate for straw-bale construction may be semi-arid, with hot summers and cold winters, but successful examples exist in a wide range of climates.

Q. What about durability/longevity?
A. The evidence provided by existing hay and straw-bale structures built by Great Plains homesteaders as early as 1903 is irrefutable - bale houses, if properly built and maintained, can have a useful lifespan of at least 90 years, even in areas where high winds are common. Specialists in earthquake-resistant design have predicted that structures with properly pinned bale walls will be unusually resistant to collapse due to earthquake-generated motion.

Q. What keeps the roof of a straw-bale building from being lifted off by high winds?
A. Some straw-bale buildings consist of a "post and beam" framework wrapped (inside or out) or infilled with bales. In this situation, the roof structure is firmly attached to the horizontal beams, which are attached to vertical posts, which are themselves fastened to the foundation. In a loadbearing bale structure, there are no vertical posts. The "beams", in this type of building, can take many forms. When taken together, the "beams" are called a "roof-bearing assembly", or RBA. The roof structure is attached to the RBA, which is itself attached to the foundation.

Q. Does the use of bales impose limitations on the building design?
A. If a framework is used to carry the roof weight, the limitations are very few. One could conceivably build a multi-storied building with straw-bale infill or wrap a huge single-story building with non-loadbearing bale walls.

However, if one wishes to use the walls to carry the roof weight, the unique properties or idiosyncrasies of bales and of bale walls must be given serious consideration. Historic experience and structural testing suggest reasonable limits on the following: 1) the maximum height of walls; 2) the maximum length of wall between buttresses or braces; 3) the individual position and width of, and the total area of, the openings in any one wall, and 4) the maximum compressive load on any square foot of wall-top area. For a detailed treatment of the constraints on the loadbearing approach, see page 31.

Where more space is required than can be comfortably provided by a single-story square or rectangle (of acceptable length), builders have turned to "bent rectangles" (e.g., L-shapes, U-shapes or designs with fully surrounded courtyards). Another strategy is to create additional living space under a "sheltering roof" (e.g., cathedral, gambrel). The use of bales does not automatically disqualify any particular roof shape. However, many builders do try to avoid an essentially flat roof surrounded on four sides by parapet walls (a style particularly popular in the southwestern U.S.). Such roofs are notorious for leaking, especially if the drain holes become plugged and the "bathtub" begins to fill up. For those willing to sacrifice the parapet wall on one side, combining three parapets with a shed roof offers a possible compromise (see *Some Standard Roof Shapes* on page 75).

Whether or not they are loadbearing, bale walls are invariably thicker than those resulting from standard frame or masonry construction. In feeling, they more resemble double adobe or rammed earth walls. Unlike earth walls, they cannot practically be left permanently exposed, but a wide choice of coverings can be used (e.g., cement-, lime-, gypsum-, or clay-based plasters, gunite, metal or vinyl siding, wood paneling or sheathing, gypsum-based panels [e.g., sheetrock, drywall]). Many bale buildings have the exterior walls surfaced differently on the inside than on the outside.

Q. What about obtaining construction insurance and a building loan convertible to a mortgage? Do such houses have normal resale value and can potential buyers get financing?
A. The early straw-bale houses were uninsured, pay-as-you-build structures, sometimes by choice, sometimes by necessity. As the technique has gained credibility with building officials, lenders and insurers, it has become easier, generally speaking, to get permits, financing and insurance.

Unfortunately, the attitude toward straw-bale construction can differ greatly from one place to another, from one company to

another and within a given company (from one region to another). Ask straw-bale homeowners in your area where they got financing or coverage.

In regard to financing, a written resource that may help you when things are looking bleak is *Empowering the Borrower* by longtime, alternative- construction guru, Eric Black (1996). Regarding insurance, an independent broker can sometimes locate a more adventurous carrier when the big guys wimp out.

The resale value of modern straw-bale homes is difficult to determine since very few have been put on the market. If, as we predict, a strong demand for pre-owned straw-bale houses develops, the hesitancy of insurers and lenders will decrease accordingly. Hot spots like the Santa Fe, New Mexico, area, Tucson, Arizona, and Crestone, Colorado, will be the places to watch.

Q. Will a straw-bale house cost less to heat and cool than a typical frame or masonry house, assuming comparable interior size, shape, ceiling insulation and solar orientation?
A. To provide more than a trivial answer to this question, we need to introduce the concept of R-values (called RSI-values where the metric system is used). These are numerical values which provide a quantitative measure of the resistance of a material or wall system to the transfer of heat through it by conduction (i.e., a measure of the degree of insulation it provides). The R-value per inch of thickness of dry, baled straw, for example, is on the order of 2.5 to 3 [RSI of 0.44 to 0.53], very close to that for fiberglass batts. Since thick house walls of dense materials (e.g., concrete, rammed earth) maintain interior comfort levels much better than their

low R-values would suggest, a calculated "effective R-value" is used to predict the actual performance of such walls.

And now, to answer the question. Since typical construction seldom provides wall-system R-values greater than 20 [RSI-3.52], a well-built, straw-bale house with walls providing R-values of from R-40 to R-50 [RSI-7.04 to RSI-8.80] (depending on surface coverings, density of bales, thickness of walls, etc.) will obviously cost less to heat and cool than a typically built home. These energy savings, which will be proportionally greater for smaller designs than for larger ones, will accrue to the owner month after month for the lifespan of the building.

Q. Since straw bales are a relatively low-mass material, will they work well in a passive solar design?

A. The major physical components of an ideal passive solar design would include south-facing glazing, adequate thermal mass (to store and release heat on a 24-hour cycle), and an insulating exterior wrap to reduce heat loss to the outside. In straw-bale construction, proper placement of high-mass materials like plaster, brick, concrete, tile, or earth materials (e.g., adobe, cob*, rammed earth) in the interior of the structure provide the needed thermal mass, while the thick, highly-insulative, straw-bale walls greatly reduce heat loss by conduction. Straw bales on the outside, earth on the inside—we win, the planet wins.

A typical cob mixture consists of clay-rich soil, sand, a good deal of straw, and water. A stiff mixture of the above ingredients is formed into bread-loaf sized blobs which are slammed down onto the foundation, and then onto the previous layer, successively, to form a wall. See Bee (1997) or Smith (1997) for comprehensive presentations of the technique.

Q. Strictly from the standpoint of maximizing the advantages and minimizing the disadvantages of straw-bale exterior walls, is there an ideal size for a simple, rectangular building?

A. This is obviously a very narrow way of looking at how big or small a building should be, but several factors point to dimensions that will provide an interior useable space of about 1200 square feet [111.5 square meters]. This size building has a ceiling area approximately equal to the internal surface area of the outside walls, so the impressive R- or RSI-value you get by stacking the bales is not overshadowed by ceiling area that one needs to insulate. At the same time, by having an interior as large as 1200 square feet [111.5 square meters], we have reached the point where the square footage of the structure's "footprint" is only 16.5% greater than that needed for a house having a 2" X 6" [about 5 cm X 15 cm] frame wall.

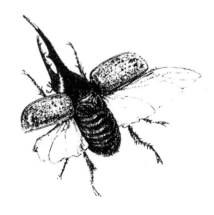

Twinecutterus nobullis

Part
One
Before You Build

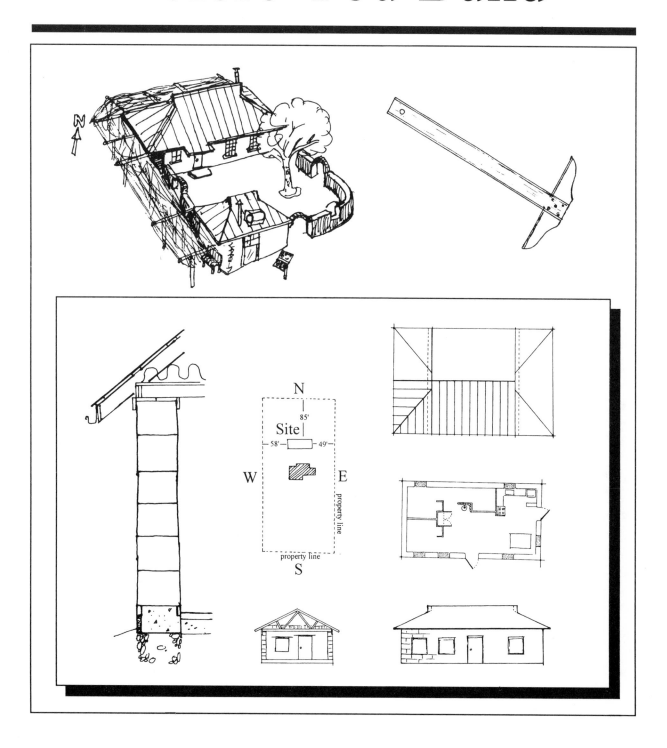

Starting with Bales

Hay versus Straw

The term "hay" is used to describe the material which results from cutting certain plants while still green and allowing them to partially dry before removing them from the field. Stored in stacks or bales until needed, this nutritive product is fed to animals.

Contrast this with "straw", the dry, dead stems of plants, generally cereal grains, that is sometimes removed from the field after the seed heads have been harvested. The majority of this low-value, nutrition-poor by-product is burned or tilled into the soil—only a small percentage of that which is available is baled. Although baled meadow hay has been used by both historic and a few modern builders, straw is the preferred (and generally cheaper) material.

Bale Options

Bales come in a variety of sizes and shapes, but those most commonly used for building are the small rectangular bales. These come with either two or three ties, and the ties may be wire, polypropylene twine or natural fiber twine. Consult the diagram (next column) for "vital statistics". Although two-tie bales are virtually always 14 inches [35.6 cm] high, three-tie bales come either 14, 15, or 16 inches [35.6, 38.1, 40.6 cm] high. Don't assume, because the 16 inch [40.6 cm] height is the most common, that your bales will necessarily come with this dimension.

Builders have generally favored polypropylene twine as a tying material because it cannot rust, but wire runs a close second. Natural fiber twine is considered a

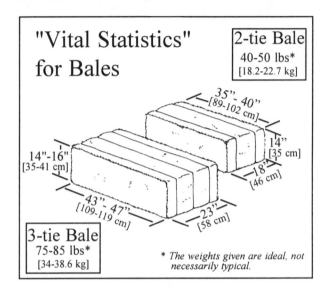

"Vital Statistics" for Bales

2-tie Bale 40-50 lbs* [18.2-22.7 kg]

35"-40" [89-102 cm]

14" [35 cm]

14"-16" [35-41 cm]

18" [46 cm]

43"-47" [109-119 cm]

23" [58 cm]

3-tie Bale 75-85 lbs* [34-38.6 kg]

* The weights given are ideal, not necessarily typical.

final resort due to its low tensile strength and susceptibility to rot. Builders have commonly used either two- or three-tie bales in non-loadbearing designs, and have used them laid both "flat" and "on edge". For designs with loadbearing bale walls, most builders try to use the more-compact, wider, three-tie bales laid "flat", rather than the narrower, two-tie bales. Successful examples do exist, however, of structures with loadbearing, two-tie bales laid "flat", and loadbearing, three-string bales laid "on edge".

The Ideal, Building-Grade Bale

This hypothetical **super-bale** would be:

• dry—the drier the better. At a moisture content below about 20% (calculated as a percentage of the total weight of the bale), virtually none of the species of fungal spores commonly present in straw can reproduce and cause the straw to break down.

• free from seed heads that would encourage rodents to inhabit the walls should the wall surfacing not be properly maintained.

• about twice as long as it is wide. Such bales, when laid "flat", will lay up with a true "running bond", where each vertical joint between two adjacent bales in a course will fall at the midpoint of the bales above and below the joint.

• made up of stems at least 10 inches [25 cm] long and which are still tubular. When a flake about 3 inches [7.6 cm] wide is separated from such a bale, it will maintain its rectangular shape when lifted and moved. **Avoid bales consisting of short, shattered stems that won't hold together as a flake or that abrade easily at the corners.** They are messy (fire hazard!), tend to lose their outside strings, and may not have fully as much structural integrity as bales with longer stems. Also, avoid bales that have been reconstituted into smaller bales from large round or rectangular bales.

• consistent in size, shape and degree of compaction with its neighbors. Such bales will make it easier to build straight, relatively smooth-surfaced walls of uniform height. This, in turn, minimizes the amount of bale-tweaking needed to remove excessive irregularity. It also decreases the amount of plaster, if this is being used, that will be needed to achieve the desired amount of wall smoothness.

• sufficiently compact for its intended use. This proves to be easier to suggest than to provide standards for. Until some inexpensive, easy-to-construct, standard device has been adopted to physically measure the degree of compaction of baled plant stems, we're stuck with using density (loosely defined as weight per unit volume) as

an easily calculated substitute for degree of compaction.

In non-loadbearing designs, the degree of compaction is much less critical, since the bales are braced against forces perpendicular to the wall surfaces by the roof-bearing framework. The code for the State of New Mexico for non-loadbearing construction requires only that the bales can be picked up by one string without deforming.

If the bale walls will be carrying the roof load, the degree of compression will affect the stiffness of the pinned walls and their resistance to wind and seismic loads. It will also influence the total amount of wall compaction resulting from a given load, per square foot, on the top of the wall and the time required for it to be completed.

This is all good to know, but still leaves us needing a way to easily determine the average "calculated density" (CD) of our bales to see if it exceeds some accepted, minimum value. The standard procedure has been to weigh a given bale and to then estimate, using a measuring tape and several small pieces of plywood, the dimensions of an "envelope rectangle" that would snugly enclose that bale. Each dimension in inches and eighths (e.g., 46-3/8"), needs then to be converted to inches and decimal inches. To do this, divide the numerator of the fractional inches by the denominator (e.g., 3 divided by 8 equals 0.375") and add this to the whole inches (e.g., 46.375"). Now multiply the converted length, width and height and divide the result by 1728 (the number of cubic inches in a cubic foot). Divide this result into the weight of the bale (in pounds) to obtain the CD in pounds per cubic foot. [Metric CD in kilograms per cubic meter = weight of bale in kg / length in m X width in m X height in m.]

The accuracy of this result depends, unfortunately, on the assumption that the bale is bone dry. The presence of moisture (i.e., liquid water) in the bale will give a falsely high result.

Moisture content is normally expressed as a percentage of the total weight of the "damp" bale, and is calculated by dividing the weight of free water in a bale by the total weight of the bale, including water, then multiplying that by 100. Thus, a 90 pound bale in which 18 pounds was due to water would have a moisture content of 20% (18 divided by 90, times 100). Conversely, if you know that this 90 pound bale has a moisture content of 20%, you know that 18 pounds of the total weight is water. The dry weight of the bale is thus 72 pounds. This is the weight you would use to determine the CD.

But how can you determine the moisture content of the bales? Most moisture meters, using a probe stuck into the bale, cannot read accurately below about 13%. However, this is well below the generally accepted upper limit for safe use in building (i.e., 20%) . If the meter indicates a maximum of 13%, it is typical to assume a moisture content of 10%. In most cases this will result in a CD that is conservatively low.

Simple lab procedures performed on samples taken from bales can also determine the moisture content very accurately, but require destroying the bales and are time-consuming and expensive.

What is needed, but not yet available, is a method for determining the degree of compaction that is independent of the moisture content and that can be performed quickly, on the building site, with an inexpensive device. Send us your ideas!

Ordering Building-Grade Bales

To custom order bales that will meet a reasonable standard for density, we must first set this standard and then translate it into simple instructions for the operator. Testing has demonstrated (see Eisenberg et al. 1993) that walls built with bales having a calculated density (CD), based on dry weight, of at least 7.0 pounds per cubic foot [112.25 kg per cubic meter], can safely carry a load of at least 360 pounds per square foot [1759 kg per square meter] without showing unacceptable compression or deformation. Using this value of 7.0, we can now determine for a given bale size, what its minimum weight should be for use in a loadbearing wall carrying no more than this 360 pounds per square foot load. We need only multiply 7.0 by the volume in cubic feet of the bale size that we want operator to produce for us (those fortunate souls using the metric system would simply multiply 112.25 by the volume of the bale in cubic meters). For example, if we ask for custom, two-tie bales that are 14" by 18" by 36", we would specify that they weigh at least 37 pounds. We get this by multiplying 14 by 18 by 36 to get the bale volume in cubic inches, dividing this by 1728 to convert to cubic feet, and then multiplying this volume by 7.0. The operator can now adjust the baler to produce bales with an average length of 36" and a weight of not less than 37 pounds.

Sources of Bales

In areas where cereal grains (e.g., wheat, oats, barley, rye, rice) or grass seeds are produced, it is often possible to buy bales cheaply in the fields or from stacks located beside the fields, but you will have to transport them. Farmers will sometimes load and deliver, but transportation is generally provided by independent truckers.

The cost per bale, bought retail in small quantities at a "feed store", is often significantly higher than the price that can be negotiated, through the feed store or the producer, for a larger quantity. Other potential sources of information on bale suppliers include state agricultural agencies, county agricultural agents, race tracks, zoos, and the summer "resource" issues of *The Last Straw*.

Flammability and Fire Retardants

Testing by a certified laboratory (see SBCA 1994) has clearly established that a straw-bale wall, while protected by plaster, is at least as fire resistant as a wood frame wall similarly protected. **Exposed straw**, however, like wood and other cellulosic materials, **will support combustion under certain circumstances**.

The time period between getting the walls up and getting them surfaced constitutes a significant window of vulnerability. This needs to be taken seriously, as several unfortunate straw-bale builders have learned the hard way, by losing their buildings to fire during the construction process (e.g., *The Last Straw*, Issue 13, page 34 and Issue 16, page 16).

The greatest potential for fire lies not in the bales, but in **loose straw** that is allowed to accumulate on the site, particularly during the wall-raising. Under windy conditions, flames will spread rapidly through a layer of dry, loose straw. Fortunately, this danger can be easily eliminated by repeatedly raking or sweeping up the loose straw, stuffing it into plastic garbage bags and storing it at a safe

distance from the building. This is an important job that even very small people can help with.

The surface of a compact bale will not normally support combustion once the "fuzz" has burned off. The least flammable, exposed-bale wall will therefore be the one with the most dense, least "fuzzy" bales. Even then, two other danger spots exist where "flakes" have been used to fill gaps between bales and where loose straw has been stuffed into the openings left where bales butt up against each other. Capping the loose straw at these locations with a mixture of straw and mud ("cob") will eliminate the danger they present.

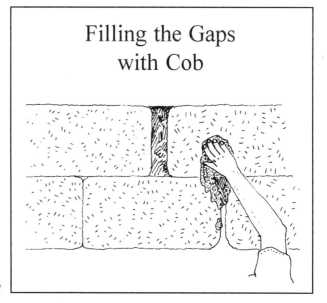

Filling the Gaps with Cob

One additional danger relates to string-tied bales stacked on edge. Flames moving up the wall can easily destroy the strings, releasing loose straw to further fuel the fire.

Another obvious way to reduce the risk of fire is to keep the work site free from all possible sources of ignition. **Activities to be avoided/prevented** would include:

- **smoking**;
- **welding** of any kind;

• **any grinding or cutting** that will produce sparks (i.e., tiny fragments of red-hot metal);

• and, **arson**.

Although there have been only a few fires for which arson has been the likely cause, it is clear that exposed straw-bale walls conjure up the possibility of fire in a way that an exposed, dimension-lumber frame does not. In situations where the risk of arson is greatest (e.g., certain inner-city neighborhoods), the builder might want to:

• put a fence around the site;

• maintain a continuous presence (human or guard dog);

• shorten the period during which the bale walls are left unsurfaced, by pre-stressing the walls (see page 73) or by using a non-loadbearing design (see page 21);

• and/or treat the bales, or bale walls, with a fire retardant chemical (see next paragraph).

Commercially available retardants like Nochar's "Fire Preventer" (call 317-573-4860) or Northeast Fireshield's "Inspecta-Shield" (call 516-563-0960) are effective but relatively expensive. For a less expensive alternative, some builders have used a saturated solution of borax and boric acid (both in granular form) dissolved in hot water. Heating the water enables more of the borax to be dissolved, and the boric acid counteracts the caustic, corrosive nature of the borax. For maximum strength, keep the water hot during both the mixing and the application. Typical mixes have involved 1 part by volume boric acid to 2 parts borax, both of which are readily available at chemical supply houses (e.g., Hills Brothers, a national chain). An additional side benefit of the borax is that it is an effective fungicide.

Aluminum sulfate (commonly called alum) has also shown promise as a simple, home-brewed fire retardant, although we could find no specific recipe to provide. If you try it and like it, send us some specifics for version three.

Fire retardant solutions have usually been applied to the bale walls with spraying equipment. The options for do-it-yourselfers include paint sprayers or power weed sprayers that are available at equipment rental centers or a hand-pressurized, backpack sprayer. Using a plasterer's "hopper gun" would allow a little clay to be added to the borax/boric acid solution. The clay, besides bonding the chemicals to the straw, has a fire retardant effect of its own. An alternative to spraying is dipping one or more surfaces of the bales into a fire retardant solution. This will provide greater penetration than spraying.

With proper precautions, such as those outlined above, you should never have to fight a fire on your building site, **but be ready to fight the fire that somehow gets started anyway**. An adequate water supply, delivered with good pressure, provides the best defense. The hoses should be long enough to reach all the way around your building, to the side furthest from the water source, without having to be run closer than about twenty feet to any wall.

Bale Composition

The straws of the common cereal grains are very similar in chemical composition to each other and to the common soft woods. They all consist mainly of cellulose, hemi-cellulose and lignin. It is far more important that the bales be dry and compact than that they be wheat rather than oats. Even Sudan grass, grass straw, bean stalks, and the stems of milo (a type of sorghum) have been baled and used successfully for building.

How Many Bales?

If you have completed your plans, including detailed wall "elevations" (i.e., vertical wall maps), you can determine very exactly how many bales you will need. The determination is often done as if there are no doors and windows, to insure that there will be some extra bales for temporary seating and for building ramps or to support scaffolding.

Even then, you may want to purposely order more than your plans suggest. You'll be far better off having too many, rather than too few. Use the extras to build benches, dog houses, accent walls, or to mulch the garden.

Meanwhile, for an **initial estimate**, use the graph below.

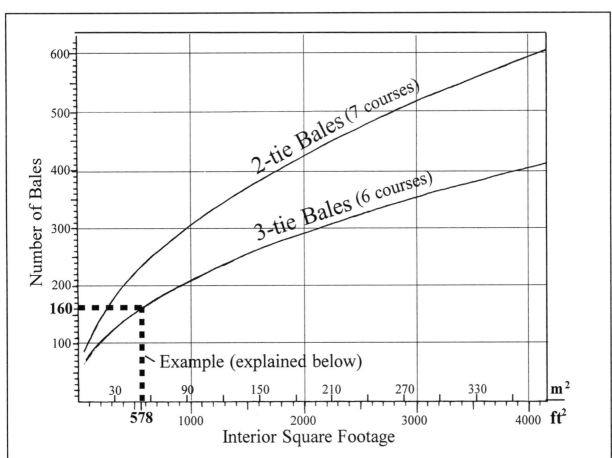

Using this graph, it is easy to **estimate the number of bales** (2-tie or 3-tie; see figure on page 15 for bale dimensions) needed to build your home. The horizontal axis is the square footage of interior space; the vertical axis the number of bales needed. We assume no openings in the walls. In the **example** shown, the interior square footage of our planned building is 578 square feet and we are using 3-tie bales. Coming straight up from 578 on the horizontal axis until we intersect with the 3-tie curve, we can then move horizontally to the left until we intersect the vertical axis at 160, the approximate number of bales needed.

Three Basic Approaches

Loadbearing

In nearly all cases, the roof weight of the historic Nebraska structures was carried entirely by the bale walls. Many of these buildings were square or modestly rectangular, with lightly-framed, true hip roofs that distributed the weight evenly, or nearly so, onto all four walls.

• Some **advantages** of the loadbearing approach include:

—greater ease of design and construction;

—possible savings of time, money, labor and materials, since no roof-bearing framework is needed;

—and, distribution of the roof and wall weight evenly along the foundation that supports the loadbearing walls.

• Some **disadvantages** include:

—certain design constraints, including the need to avoid very heavy roof systems (details, on page 31);

—the need for dense, uniform bales, laid "flat"; (This density criteria, combined with their smaller width, usually precludes the use of two-tie bales in loadbearing designs.)

—the need to wait an indeterminate period of time (generally, 3 to 10 weeks) for the bales to compress in response to the weight of the roof/insulation/ceiling system, unless your tie-down system can pull the RBA down mechanically (see page 73 for one option);

—and, the possibility that very heavy live loads (wet snow, herds of elephants, etc.) could cause the wall-surfacing materials to buckle outward. To our knowledge, however, this has never happened.

Non-Loadbearing

Many of the modern bale-walled structures have been built using an arrangement of vertical elements (generically called posts) and horizontal elements (beams) to carry the entire weight of the roof/insulation/ceiling system. The bottom bales carry only the weight of the bales above them. The bale walls provide insulation and the matrix onto which surfacing materials (e.g., plaster, siding) are attached. Typical frameworks have consisted of various combinations of 2"x4" [5X10 cm] and other dimension lumber, glue-lam beams, rough cut timber posts and beams, peeled logs, metal elements, and concrete columns and bond beams.

• Some **advantages** of the non-loadbearing approach include:

—greater familiarity, and therefore acceptability, to building officials, lenders and insurers;

—provision, by the roofed framework, of a dry shaded place for storing materials, including bales; (This enables flexible scheduling and working even when it's raining, or the sun is intense.)

—the possibility, since the framework is non-compressive, of surfacing the walls as soon as they are up;

—the possibility of using the typically less-dense, two-tie bales or less-dense-than-normal three-tie bales, and of laying the bales "on edge";

—a reduction in constraints on the size, number and placement of openings;

—and, freedom from certain other design constraints (e.g., length of unbuttressed walls, roof weight).

• Some **disadvantages** include:
—the expenditure of extra time, money, labor and materials to create the framework; (For an owner-builder, this means a more complex design challenge and the need for skills they may not have.)
—and, the need to create a more complex foundation system that can carry both the bale walls and the concentrated loads transferred to it by the vertical "posts".

Hybrid

The distinction between the first two general approaches we have described is specifically "structural". The *Hybrid Approach*, as we define it, does include buildings that are "structural" hybrids, but we will also include here a variety of building types that are both significantly straw-bale, and are "combinations" (i.e., hybrids), in other ways. By its nature, a hybrid structure often requires extra thought during the design process. Draw it, model it, get a "second opinion", and still expect to have to think on your feet once you get started.

For descriptive purposes we can separate hybrids into three, somewhat overlapping, categories: "structural", "compositional", and "temporal".

• **"Structural" hybrids** are those in which both compressive straw-bale walls and non-compressive walls/frameworks, made with other materials, carry roof weight. Combining both of these wall types in a design can release you from some of the constraints, or disadvantages, of each. In a single story building this could mean, for example, a central adobe wall carrying half of the roof load, with the other half shared by two exterior loadbearing straw-bale walls. Or it could mean a shed-roofed building with lots of windows in a "post-and-beam" framework on the south side, and a loadbearing bale wall on the north side.

Designs of this type must take into consideration the fact that the bale walls will compress, lowering the RBA and changing the pitch of the roof. In a building involving a heavy roof system, long rafter spans and spongy bales, the problem could be significant.

In a full, two-story structure, this could mean, for the first story, an engineered, "post-and-beam" framework (wrapped or infilled with bales) topped with a deck. Upon this deck, for a second story, could sit full-height, loadbearing straw-bale walls capped with a roof. Or, it could mean a full, designed-to be-lived-in basement, with a loadbearing bale building on top of it.

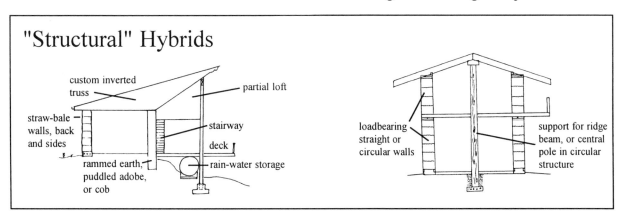

"Structural" Hybrids

custom inverted truss — straw-bale walls, back and sides — partial loft — stairway — deck — rammed earth, puddled adobe, or cob — rain-water storage — loadbearing straight or circular walls — support for ridge beam, or central pole in circular structure

• **"Compositional" hybrids** are those in which the "combination" is primarily that of different materials. This could mean, for example, a building with a gable roof carried by two straw-bale walls, where the end walls are an infill of cordwood and colored bottles.

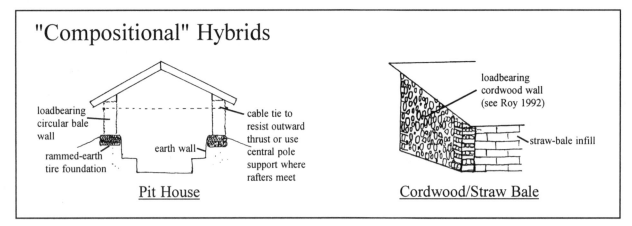

"Compositional" Hybrids

loadbearing circular bale wall

cable tie to resist outward thrust or use central pole support where rafters meet

rammed-earth tire foundation

earth wall

Pit House

loadbearing cordwood wall (see Roy 1992)

straw-bale infill

Cordwood/Straw Bale

• **"Temporal" hybrids** are those in which the old and the new are combined. One example would be a **retrofit**. You could upgrade an **old**, uninsulated masonry house, that's been sitting in some urban neighborhood wasting megawatts of energy, by installing **new windows and doors**, by adding enough **new ceiling insulation** to reach the regional standard for super-insulation, and by installing **new "outsulation"**, in the form of a bale wrap of the exterior walls. Here's the ideal combination of **great insulation on the outside** and **thermal mass on the inside**! For tips on energy-efficient renovation, see Marshall and Ague (1981) or Harland (1994). If you plan to replace old systems, appliances, or components (e.g., windows) with more energy-efficient ones, consult Wilson and Morrill (1996).

This category would also include a straw-bale **addition**; that is, a **new** straw-bale segment added to an **"old"** structure built with some other material. The Department of Housing and Urban Development (a.k.a. HUD) has a special, 203K loan program for "renovations" that has accepted straw-bale construction for additions.

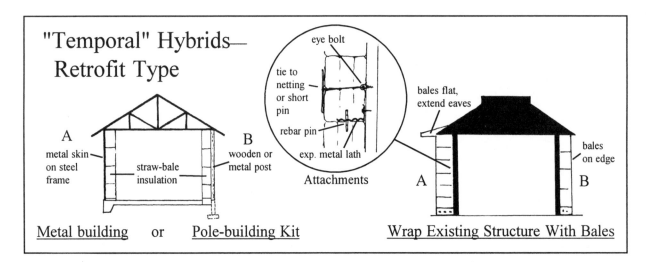

"Temporal" Hybrids—
Retrofit Type

eye bolt

tie to netting or short pin

rebar pin

exp. metal lath

Attachments

A
metal skin on steel frame

straw-bale insulation

B
wooden or metal post

Metal building   or   Pole-building Kit

bales flat, extend eaves

bales on edge

A

B

Wrap Existing Structure With Bales

Pay-As-You-Go "Structural" Hybrid

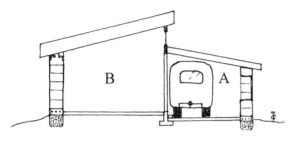

Phase 0 - Live in trailer, saving money to build a hybrid straw-bale home.

Phase 1 - Build space A to shade trailer, leaving one end temporarily plugged with bales.

Phase 2 - Save more money.

Phase 3 - Build Space B.

Phase 4. Unstack temporary end wall, remove trailer, replace end wall and finish.

Phase 5. Sell the trailer to someone who wants to do what you just finished doing.

Our Model as a "Structural" Hybrid

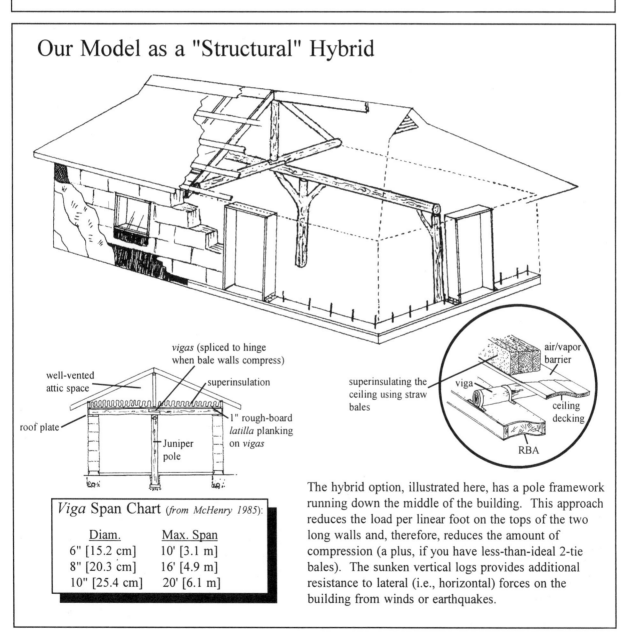

vigas (spliced to hinge when bale walls compress)

well-vented attic space

superinsulation

roof plate

Juniper pole

1" rough-board *latilla* planking on *vigas*

superinsulating the ceiling using straw bales

air/vapor barrier

viga

ceiling decking

RBA

Viga Span Chart *(from McHenry 1985)*:	
Diam.	Max. Span
6" [15.2 cm]	10' [3.1 m]
8" [20.3 cm]	16' [4.9 m]
10" [25.4 cm]	20' [6.1 m]

The hybrid option, illustrated here, has a pole framework running down the middle of the building. This approach reduces the load per linear foot on the tops of the two long walls and, therefore, reduces the amount of compression (a plus, if you have less-than-ideal 2-tie bales). The sunken vertical logs provides additional resistance to lateral (i.e., horizontal) forces on the building from winds or earthquakes.

Developing a Plan

The Superinsulation Strategy

We could have accurately subtitled this book "the novice builder's guide to creating affordable, **superinsulated house-walls**, and a bit more". Although such walls are a necessary element in a superinsulated house, they do not, by themselves, give you one.

For those of you planning to build where long periods of very cold or hot weather are the norm, a **superinsulated house** will provide significant energy savings. For in-depth coverage of the superinsulation strategy, consult Nisson and Dutt (1985).

Four important components of such a house are:

• a carefully defined "thermal envelope" that separates the "climate-controlled" spaces from the "uncontrollable" outside;

• sufficient insulation, carefully installed (typically R-30 to R-40 [RSI 5.3 to 7.0] for walls; R-35 to R-65 [RSI 6.2 to 11.4] for ceilings; whole-window U-values of 0.37 or lower [U metric values of 2.1 or lower]);

• air tightness, with controlled ventilation that often includes an air-to-air exchanger;

• and, a modest amount of south-facing glazing to provide solar gain to replace the small amount of heat lost through the thermal envelope.

A Different Way Of Building

Straw-bale construction encourages us to explore a different philosophy of building, one which includes imperatives like those listed below:

• Use passive heating and cooling systems to the extent possible (EPA 1992, Givoni 1994, Anderson 1996).

• Design to enhance eventual expansion, but build now only what is enough for now.

• Build accretionally, with final inspections as each major stage is completed. For example, complete the basic core, with kitchen, bathroom and a multipurpose living space. Move legally into this and then add a bedroom. Future additions might be a master bedroom and bath or an office space. See the drawing of the "model" structure on page 42 regarding window frames that convert easily into door frames to provide access to additions.

• Make a gradual transition from a small, actually mobile, trailer, to a finished straw-bale home. (See the drawing on page 24.)

• Design your spaces to be wheelchair accessible. Sooner or later, someone will thank you for this foresight. For guidance in this area, see Wylde et al. (1993).

• Keep the design simple, the size small (keep asking yourself if you've drawn more than enough), and the storage inventive (utilizing otherwise dead spaces). For suggestions, consult Metz (1991), Brown (1993), Smith (1995), and Dickinson (1996). Make the spaces multi-functional, and the partitions easily movable. In temperate climates, consider a fully-climatized core, with zones around it that become increasingly less enclosed as you move outward.

• Use scrounged/recycled "green" and materials where possible (see Harris [ongoing], Stulz and Mukerji 1993, Pearson

1989 and 1996, Good Wood Alliance 1996, Mumma 1997).

• Choose materials with the lowest potential toxicity (Bower 1993, Marinelli and Bierman-Lytle 1995, Venolia 1995, Steen and Steen 1997c). If the structure will house someone who is environmentally hypersensitive, see CMHC (1995).

• Do all or part of the building yourself (or as a family effort).

• Pay for the building as you go, as you can. Imagine no mortgage payments and, particularly, no interest payments. That would be another galaxy, and a kinder, gentler one at that.

You will find additional philosophical underpinnings for these imperatives in Alexander (1979), Kern (1975), and in Henry David Thoreau's classic, *Walden.*

Site Selection Considerations

The term "site selection" seems to automatically conjure up the idea of locating and buying a piece of land out in the middle of some beautiful chunk of uninhabited country and building a new house on it. We would ask you to instead consider **staying put**, "outsulating" your existing home with bales, and/or adding onto it with bales, or razing it and replacing it with a straw-bale house, or building on a vacant lot within an existing community (see Sanders 1993).

Consider helping to make an urban neighborhood more whole, more vital and more healthy, rather than unintentionally making a rural ecosystem less so. Where you build can be as important to planetary sustainability as what you build with. As Nadav Malin (1995a), of *Environmental Building News*, sees it, "...Where we choose

to build will dictate, in many cases, transportation patterns. Energy use and pollution from driving cars far outweighs the energy use in buildings, so even the most efficient building can be undermined if the occupants are set up for long commutes...Building location also affects the wildlife and habitat of its immediate surroundings. Remote, self-sufficient, off-the-grid homes are often the first intrusions into pristine wilderness areas, but they are rarely the last."

When you have finally chosen your lot or parcel, you will need to select the specific spot for your building(s). On a small lot, you may have little latitude in positioning your building. Given a larger piece of land, careful study of the whole piece will probably reveal several possible sites where the footprint of your "destruction zone" will do the least damage to the land and the other living things that will share this land with you. All construction involves destruction, but why damage a really beautiful spot, with great wildlife habitat, when you can pick an already damaged, or less healthy site, that you can restore to health after building on it? The landscaping you later do around your home can provide both energy-saving seasonal shade, and habitat for the wildlife whose land claim predates yours. Having identified a number of such potential sites, one can then try measuring each site against a list of characteristics of the "ideal" building site for the type of design you envision.

For a "floor-on-earth", single-level design, here are some possible characteristics:

• The views are attractive to you (could mean vast or restricted), and don't destroy some neighbor's views.

• Access to the site is reasonable.

• There is a reasonably flat area big

enough for the building.

• If the site has a slope, it is generally toward the south (unless solar gain is not an issue.

• The drainage pattern will not present any unplanned-for difficulties.

• The position of the site in the general landscape will ameliorate the least attractive aspects of the climate rather than accentuate them.

• Winter sun, for passive solar gain, reaches the site.

• The geology of site is such as to minimize problems and expenses related to site preparation and foundation design and construction.

Although none of your sites may exhibit all the desired features, this exercise will enable you to compare them and develop a ranking that reflects how strongly you feel about the various "ideal" characteristics. Valuable aids for this process include Lynch and Hack (1984), Mollison and Slay (1988), Walters (1991), and McHarg (1995).

Preliminary Conceptual Design

After coming up with some loose, informal, preliminary sketches, but before spending time developing detailed plans, you may want to initially consider some relevant, generic issues. You may also want to now involve an architect or designer in the process, rather than forging on alone. If so, shop around— talk to former clients, explore philosophy, find someone whose creative ego won't bury your input.

Very early in the process, check on the availability of good bales in your area. When you get information from potential sources of three-tie bales, be sure to determine what different heights they offer. Although they are most commonly sixteen inches (40.6 cm) high, you cannot safely make any assumptions. Designing for one height and having them deliver bales with another, can spoil your whole day. **Don't procrastinate!** For a loadbearing structure, there is nothing more important than acquiring the right bales. It may take months. Start shopping early!!!

If only two-tie bales are available, **seriously** consider using the non-loadbearing approach. A possible exception would be for a small building with walls no higher than about eight feet (2.44 m), if you can locate, or have made for you, bales that are sufficiently compact to carry roof load. You could even consider doing what the authors did for a project in Mongolia, i.e., using a homemade, lever-arm bale press to further compress the bales prior to retying them.

At the same time, be exploring the code situation for your state, county or municipality. Don't assume anything! Should a building code apply to the type of building you propose, at the specific location you propose to build it, you must then decide whether to do the building legally, or to "bootleg" it. Before choosing the latter, consider carefully the consequences of being discovered.

In working with your building department, it will help to provide them with information about this technique as early as possible. The *Straw Bale House* (Steen et al. 1994) has proven very helpful in convincing code enforcers that these houses are demonstrably durable, and do not endanger the health and safety of their occupants.

Other effective tools for educating your building officials are:

• the video called *Straw Bale Code*

Testing;
• Issue No. 14 of *The Last Straw*, which focuses on getting straw-bale construction into the mainstream;
• and, David Eisenberg's working paper, *Straw-Bale Construction and the Building Codes*.

These materials are available from various sources, including:
• *Black Range Films* (888-252-5652);
• *The Development Center for Appropriate Technology* (520-624-6628);
• and, *Out On Bale—By Mail* (520-624-1673).

Bend over backwards not to develop an adversarial relationship with your building officials. This doesn't mean being a wimp and letting them bluff you into thinking you can't do something that you believe is legitimate. It does mean doing your homework (get and study the appropriate zoning descriptions and code sections) and making them aware, in a non-threatening way, that you have done so. Assure them that you want to work with them to do something that is safe and legal, and provide testing data as backup. Put them in touch with building officials in jurisdictions that have already issued permits. If necessary, utilize the existing appeals process. **Good-natured, informed perseverance is a formidable tool.**

For help in working effectively with building codes and officials, see Eisenberg (1995) and Hageman (1994). Your local building department will have a copy of the code they use, for you to read on the premises.

As part of this preliminary design work, you can also begin considering possible foundation options. Relevant background information may include hydrologic data (e.g., floodplain designations), climatic data (e.g.,

depth to frost line), geologic data (e.g., depth to, and nature of bedrock), and soil data (e.g., permafrost conditions, slope stability, bearing capability). For some specific options to consider, see *The Loadbearing Option*, *Step 1* and Issue No. 16 of *The Last Straw*. Explore the possibility of having perimeter insulation, perhaps with a termite shield, as part of your foundation system.

Structural Implications of Openings in Bale Walls

When we stack and pin bale walls, we create a sort of "fabric", whose strength and stiffness is greatest when no openings are made in it. Skylights don't affect this "fabric", but doors and windows will. As general rule, it is probably not wise to have the total area of openings in any wall, unless it has a braced framework, exceed fifty percent of the total wall surface area.

Another general rule followed by most modern bale builders is to place no opening closer than one and a half bale lengths to any corner or to another opening.

Wide openings require a stronger, heavier lintel or roof-bearing assembly (RBA) to bridge the opening, or a beefier, loadbearing frame to carry the roof and/or wall weight sitting above it. For these reasons, openings are often made higher and narrower, rather than lower and wider (see *The Loadbearing Option, Step 2*, for details). If the climate dictates a large amount of south-facing glass, it may be wise to consider using frame or post-and-beam in the south wall.

Idiosyncrasies of Bales as a Construction Material

The intent of this section is to help you to start "thinking like a bale". Such thinking can generate a design process based on what these "fuzzy, squishy bricks" really are comfortable doing. A design process based on "thinking like a bale" will honor the unique qualities of bales, and result in buildings which reflect these qualities in their form and feeling.

Structural engineers involved with the revival tell us that bales are unlike any building material that they normally encounter. The basic technique resembles masonry, but masonry units (adobe blocks, fired clay bricks, concrete blocks, etc.) are brittle, non-compressive and fail catastrophically when loaded past their limit. Wood frame construction has some inherent flexibility, but is essentially non-compressive under vertical loading until failure occurs. Bale walls are flexible, compressive and relatively elastic, responding to loading by gradual deformation rather than sudden, brittle failure. For an excellent guide to structural design for straw-bale buildings, see King (1996).

The structural uniqueness of bales is only the first in a long list of unusual characteristics for you to consider as you begin the design/build process:

• In a given area, bales are usually produced during a short period and the supply for the next twelve months is fixed at this point. Everyone doing straw-bale buildings in your area will be diminishing this fixed supply, so it makes sense to buy and build soon after the new batch becomes available.

An additional concern is the regional availability of compact, three-tie bales versus the typically looser, less compact, two-tie bales. Rather than have three-tie bales brought in from great distance, you may decide to have customized, denser-than-normal, two-tie bales produced locally to meet your needs.

• A load of bales, even if all have come from the same field and from the same piece of baling equipment (baler) with the same operator, may show considerable variability in dimensions (primarily length), degree of compaction and moisture content.

• Even a single bale is not the same throughout (i.e., is not homogeneous). This has to do with the way in which the stems are folded or cut inside the baler and to their orientation within the eventual bale. The cut side of a bale often has a slightly rippled appearance and exposes the cut, tubular ends of the stems. The folded edge looks "fuzzy" and tends to shed loose straw easily when rubbed. In compressional testing of two-tie bales at Washington State University, the cut edge of the bales compressed more easily than the folded edge (for more information, contact Chris Stafford at 360-379-8541). When building a loadbearing wall with these bales, you would want to have all the cut edges out, in one course, and then all the folded edges out, in the next course, and so forth.

A different kind of non-homogeneity is evident when you try to drive things like stakes, dowels, or rebar pins into the different surfaces of a bale. Assuming a bale laid flat, the ease of penetration is greatest for the sides, somewhat less for the top or bottom, and significantly less for the ends. Experiment with your batch of bales, and then size things accordingly and sharpen them as needed.

• Bales can come tied with a number of different materials, including rustable, non-galvanized wire, polypropylene twine and a variety of natural fiber twines. Our general concerns must be that the tie material be strong, resistant to rust or rot where exposed repeatedly to damp plaster, and not attractive to rodents. Even if the bales are being laid flat (so that the ties are within the wall), the ties will be exposed where bale ends form a corner and, to a lesser extent, where bales butt against a door or window frame. If wire-tied bales are being used, backup ties of galvanized wire or polypropylene twine can be added before bales are laid at such locations, or the exposed wires can be spray painted with a rust-inhibiting paint. In general, polypropylene twine is favored over regular baling wire by many builders and fiber-tied bales are avoided.

• If simplicity and speed of stacking is a major goal, the design should involve only full and half bales. This is possible only if the bales are about twice as long as they are wide and if all openings are some whole-number multiple of half of the effective bale length (see *Finalizing the Design* on page 34).

• Under normal circumstances, the only **enemies** that the bales have are the ever-present fungi. Even these are harmless if the bales remain dry, but in the presence of sufficient, liquid moisture the enzymes they produce can gradually break down the straw. **The contract that you make with your bale walls to protect them from water (i.e., liquid water), is irrevocable.** The consequences of failure to live up to the contract are considerable, especially in a loadbearing design. An unsurfaced wall, whose top is protected, can survive repeated wettings, as long as the water can quickly be removed by evaporation. That same straw, however, if kept wet for a sufficient length of time at temperatures above a certain level, will turn into a non-structural, slimy mush. Under wet, humid conditions, you may need to wrap the whole exterior with a waterproof, preferably breathable, material until you are ready to put in place the "permanent" surfacing. So, are you willing to commit the time, energy, materials, and maintenance needed to ensure that your bales are properly protected, from the time of delivery until the building they go into is ready for recycling? If not, a more water-tolerant building material may be a wiser, safer choice for you.

• To our knowledge, all successful, purely loadbearing bale-wall designs to date have been limited to a single story, and the bales have almost without exception been laid flat. However, some single-story designs have used a sheltering gable, gambrel, or hipped roof to provide additional living space. And, hybrid designs (see page 22) offer the possibility of even three livable levels (e.g., basement, first floor, and space under the roof). For designs of this type, where structural considerations loom large, you would be well-advised to have an engineer review, or even put their stamp on, your design.

• Finally, bales can be easily (1) **divided** to create custom bales of various lengths and shapes, (2) **sculpted** to create rounded corners or edges, wall niches and *bas-relief* decorative elements, and (3) **bent** for use in curved walls.

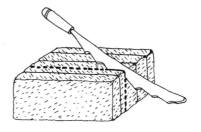

Generic Constraints for Loadbearing Design

There is agreement, among those most involved in the design of structures with loadbearing bale walls, that there are some limits regarding how far one can safely push this material. There is not agreement, however, as to exactly what those limits are. What we will do here is list a number of areas where constraints seem justified, and provide quantitative values taken from the straw-bale code presently in effect in the City of Tucson and in Pima County, both in Arizona (available from *Out On Bale—By Mail*, at 520-624-1673, or *DCAT* at 520-624-6628). This code provides a "prescriptive standard" for loadbearing straw-bale construction. Anyone within this code jurisdiction willing to build as the code "prescribes", using the techniques described (or acceptable alternatives) and staying within certain numerical limits, can get a permit without the stamp of a registered architect or engineer. Although further testing and experience may lead to changes in the prescribed techniques and to less restrictive numerical limits, the present version does provide conservative guidelines for decision-making.

A list of areas where constraints seem justified would include:

• **Maximum moisture content** at time of installation—20% of the total weight of the bale

• **Minimum calculated dry density**—7.0 pounds per cubic foot [112.25 kg per cubic meter].

• **Nominal minimum bale wall thickness**—14 inches [35.6 cm].

• **Maximum number of stories**—one.

• **Maximum wall height**— "...the bale portion shall not exceed a height-to-width ratio of 5.6 : 1 (for example, the maximum height for the bale portion of a 23 inch [58 cm] thick wall would be 10 feet - 8 inches [3.27 m]), unless...".

• **Maximum unsupported wall length** (i.e., unbraced or unbuttressed)—"The ratio of unsupported wall length to thickness, for bale walls, shall not exceed, 13:1 (for a 23 inch [58 cm] thick wall, the maximum unsupported length allowed is 25 feet [7.54 m], unless..."

• **Maximum compressive loads**—"The allowable vertical load (live and dead load) on the top of loadbearing bale walls shall not exceed 360 pounds per square foot (1759 kg per square meter) and shall act at center of the wall." This number controls how far apart the loadbearing walls can be, given a prescribed live load and a given combination of roof-bearing assembly (RBA), roof, ceiling insulation and ceiling. For a specific live load, the combination of a lightweight RBA (made possible by using loadbearing door and window frames) and a lightweight roof / ceiling system will enable the roof to span a greater distance, while still not exceeding the allowable load. For Tucson, Arizona, given the prescribed "live load" of 20 pounds per square foot [97.7 kg per square meter], and a typical wooden RBA/roof/insulation/ceiling system weighing about 15 pounds per square foot [73.3 kg per square meter], the maximum allowable span, as influenced by the roof shape, will be on the order of 25 to 30 feet [7.6 to 9.1 m].

• **Maximum area of openings**— "Openings in exterior bale walls shall not exceed 50 percent of the total wall area, based on interior dimensions, where the wall is providing resistance to lateral loads unless..." Openings do decrease a wall's resistance to lateral forces, particularly those being applied horizontally and parallel to the wall. In addition, if these openings are spanned by lintels or an RBA acting as a lintel, any compressive load will be concentrated solely on the columns of bales between the openings.

Moisture Protection Strategies

The matter of how to protect the straw from liquid moisture that may reach it in a variety of ways should not be treated lightly. Even formulating the right questions is difficult, and the answers are very specific to the local climate and even micro-climate. In any case, it makes sense to prevent water from reaching the bottom course of bales from below, or from the exterior, and to provide a waterproof drape at window sills and at the top of all walls. A review of the "building science" literature on moisture protection reveals significant disagreement among the "experts", and not just on the picky details. Wood, which is chemically similar to straw, is also subject to water damage. This means that longtime, conventional builders in your area can provide relevant advice. The written resources range from popular magazine articles (with oversimplified, cookbook answers) to scholarly texts that will panic and confuse all but the engineers among us (and sometimes them, too). We can recommend Gibson (1994) for an overview, and Issue No. 8 of *The Last Straw* for a variety of opinions. For overall coverage of moisture in buildings, see Lstiburek and Carmody (1993). For moisture-related, cold climate strategies, see ACHP (1995) and Lstiburek (1997).

Mechanical and Electrical Systems, Et Cetera

Before starting to develop a more final floor plan, decide how you will deal with your needs for the following:

• Water (water harvesting [Pacey and Cullis 1986]? well [Burns 1997]? etc.).

• Electricity (grid? stand-alone PV? wind? water? (see Potts 1993, Strong 1994).

• Transportation (interior space for vehicles, including bicycles? 220V charging station for electric vehicle?).

• Gas or LPG (butane or propane).

• Disposal/usage of "wastewater" (composting toilets [see Jenkins 1994, Van der Ryn 1995, ARCHIBIO 1995a]? artificial wetlands [Reed et al. 1994]? gray water [Ludwig 1994]?).

• Space heating (passive/active mix? radiant floor [Luttrell 1985, Siegenthaler 1995]? wood stove? etc.).

• Daylighting (gravity operated skylight/ vent [see Reynolds 1991, page 151]? RBA that includes vertical clerestory windows [see The *Last Straw*, Issue No. 4, page 6]? commercial or homemade light tubes?).

• Cooling (venting? evaporative cooler? cooling tower?) (see Lechner 1991, Cook 1989).

• Mechanical ventilation and/or air exchanging (see Bower 1995).

• Food production (e.g., attached sunspace/ growspace [see Clegg and Watkins 1987]).

Such decisions may heavily influence certain aspects of the floor plan(s) and roof shape. A decision to rely heavily on rooftop water harvesting could, for example, lead to incorporating the storage containers into the structure as loadbearing elements and/or as thermal mass. It might also suggest including generous roof overhangs or porches to increase the harvesting surface and a simple roof design that can be easily equipped with gutters.

Developing a Building Plan

Here's where you finally get down to the nitty-gritty of developing the building plan(s). You aren't likely to forget to provide spaces for cooking, eating, excreting, bathing, sleeping, lovemaking, socializing and relaxing. However, don't forget to design in space for traffic and air flow, various kinds of storage, a home office, your mechanical systems (space and water heating and cooling/ventilation, appliances [esp. washer/dryer], etc.). As mentioned earlier, consider building additional small buildings later as needs change or letting a single structure grow over time by pre-planned additions.

Even if you eventually plan to sell your house, don't let "resale" considerations bludgeon you into creating one-plan-fits-all, generic blah. Let your instincts and creativity be reflected in a design that delights you and yours, while not making it so personal a "glove" that it cannot comfortably serve anyone but you.

Sources that we have found helpful for the design process are Alexander (1977), Taylor (1983), Cecchettini et al. (1989), Day (1990), Jackson (1990), Brown (1993), and Connell (1993).

Site Preparation

This step involves whatever modification of the site is necessary in order to be able to lay out the building you have designed and create the foundations. A time-honored resource for this step is Roskind (1983). For a flat site this may be as simple as scraping the surface to remove vegetation, loose soil and roots. If the site slopes, varying amounts of cutting and filling can be done by hand, or with machinery, to create a level pad large enough

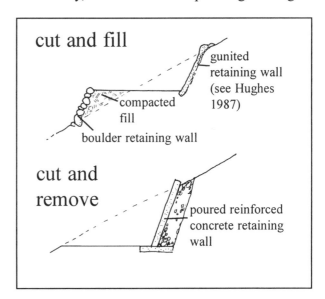

to put the structure on.

Any fill soil must be adequately compacted as it is put in place to insure that the material will not later settle under the weight of the building (see Monahan 1986). Steep cut and fill slopes will need retention and/or stabilization (see Erickson 1989). If the bale structure is to sit on a wood deck supported by posts or piers (a common response to steeply sloped sites), one need only completely clear the area where excavation for the posts will be done.

It makes sense to try to finish the site preparation before finalizing the design, because problems encountered during the site preparation may suggest major modifications in the shape of the building or in the foundation system initially favored.

Finalizing The Design

This part of the process includes a number of important, sometimes overlapping, steps. The process is complex, nonlinear and full of tradeoffs and interrelationships. The steps we list are only arguably in chronological order. Also, for you, the list may be incomplete or contain steps that are unnecessary. Consider it a checklist that you can add to or subtract from. For a non-loadbearing design, the list would also include considerations related to the "framework".

Having said all that, here they are:

• **Make a final decision on foundation and floor design.** This may include decisions about how, if at all, you will insulate under the floor (whether it is on grade or on a deck) and around the perimeter of your foundation.

• **Finalize the floor plan based on approximate bale length and a bale layout for the first and second courses.** For uncomplicated bale layouts that use only full and half bales and that give you the maximum overlap in your "running bond", you will need bales that are essentially twice as long as they are wide. This is fortunately the case with almost all three-tie bales. You will also have to base the size of all your openings on the half-bale module (i.e., a half bale wide, a full bale wide, one and a half bales wide, etc.). Any extra space left on either side of a standard door or window can be used to create angled openings, as shown in the diagram on page 56, middle right.

If the length is more than twice the width, as is common with two-tie bales, the seam between two adjacent bales in the same course will not be located over the midpoint of the bale below. This means that custom bales, that are not half bales, will be needed on either side of doors and windows. Also,

with the type of layout shown top right, the length of the first course of the walls will be different from that of the second course. To avoid problems in this case, always use the longer of the two dimensions when determining the final dimensions of the foundation. You can easily increase the shorter dimension with flakes.

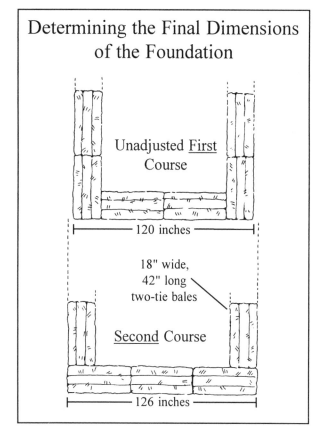

Determining the Final Dimensions of the Foundation

Unadjusted First Course

|← 120 inches →|

18" wide, 42" long two-tie bales

Second Course

|← 126 inches →|

We strongly recommend that you initially model only the first course of your proposed floor plan, using "mini-bales" that are accurately scaled for at least the two horizontal dimensions. Do the layout as if there were going to be no door openings. This will enable you to quickly see which of the layout options will give you the shape you want and the amount of interior space that you need. Then, next to this layout, model the layout of the second course, and compare the length of each wall in the first course layout, with that of the same wall in the second layout. This will show you whether you have one of the potentially problematic layouts mentioned above. Dominoes work beautifully for experimenting with possible bale layouts, if your bales will be about twice as long as they are wide. Otherwise, you can cut properly scaled shapes from various materials (e.g., cardboard boxes).

Once you have made a final decision on the bale layout for your floor plan, you can work out the width and location of doors and windows. Then make a sketch of the first course layout to record these decisions.

• **Finalize the exact dimensions of the foundation**, using an assumed bale length or a measured effective bale length. If the approximate upper limit on bale length is known, for the specific bales to be used, you can finalize the foundation dimensions using the chosen bale layout and this length. For three-tie bales, a four-foot [1.22 m] module is often used. Since few bales will approach this upper length limit, occasional flakes of loose straw will have to be used to fill small gaps as the bales are laid up. This is quickly and easily done and does not significantly weaken the walls.

Another common approach, if you are lucky enough to already have your bales, is to determine the "effective bale length". This is done by arranging ten, randomly selected bales butted snugly end to end in a straight line. With short boards held vertically against the ends of the arrangement, the distance between the inside surfaces of the two boards is measured and divided by ten. The resulting number, in decimal inches or meters, is the "effective bale length". Seasoned builders often add a quarter of an inch to provide a little cushion. The halved "effective bale

length" can also be used to finalize the width of openings. Bales can also be stacked in wall-high vertical columns to determine the "effective bale height". This figure is useful in finalizing door and window frame heights.

You should now prepare scaled drawings (where a certain distance as measured on the drawing equals a certain actual distance) of the bale layout for courses one and two. Except for the presence of window and doorway openings, all odd-numbered courses will be repeats of course one and all even-numbered courses will mirror course two. A scale of one-quarter inch equals one foot is commonly used in countries not using the metric system.

• **Create sketches of each wall (a.k.a. elevations)**, showing all courses and the location of each bale and all openings. You can use these drawings a little later when building your model

• **Select a roof shape.** In all probability, you will have already been comparing the various options for roof shapes (see the drawings on page 75), weighing a variety of factors related to cost, climate, esthetics, regional styles. etc. But now you've got to pick a favorite to try on your model, as you proceed to the next step.

• **Make a model**. Architects and building professionals are trained to effectively use two-dimensional drawings to represent three-dimensional buildings. For the rest of us ordinary mortals, models can reveal a world of problems and solutions. Nearly true-scale micro-bales can be purchased from craft supply stores. Exactly true-scale bales can be handmade from 1/2" [1.3 cm] or 1" [2.5 cm] expanded polystyrene insulation board (the high-density variety cuts more cleanly) or wood. These enable you to build a scale model of your building on the kitchen table and get most of the glitches out of the design before things get too real (see Feirer 1986).

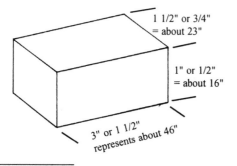

To-Scale, Styrofoam or Wooden Three-tie Mini-bales for Modeling*

1 1/2" or 3/4" = about 23"

1" or 1/2" = about 16"

3" or 1 1/2" represents about 46"

* For two-tie mini-bales: 1" or 1/2" = about 14"; 1 1/4" or 5/8" = about 18"; 2 9/16" or 1 3/16" = about 36". For metric system users: have the thickness of your foamboard equal the bale height.

The individual "bales" can be stacked and pinned (with glue, toothpicks or the equivalent), and the RBA and structural roof elements (e.g., rafters, trusses) can be modeled with balsa wood purchased from a store providing art or hobby modeling supplies.

A different, faster option for modeling the bale walls is to use correctly dimensioned pieces of 1" [2.5 cm] thick insulation board to represent whole walls. The seams between the bales are represented by a grid of lines drawn onto the wall panels.

Another option, for those of us who are "three-dimensionally challenged", is the "cybermodel". Software programs abound that enable you and your trusty computer to reduce your two-dimensional, architectural visions to bits of bytes, or whatever they are. The computer can then create a three-dimensional model that can be viewed on the screen of your monitor from various angles, from both within and without. One piece of software

which has been successfully used for modeling straw-bale "cyberhomes" is 3-D Home Architect (manufactured by Broderbund).

• **Finalize the design of the roof/ceiling system, including the choice of RBA.** Having modeled one or more options for roof shape, and having made your final choice, you can now work out the rest of the details related to the larger roof/insulation/ceiling RBA system.

• **Finalize the elevations.** This includes finalizing the location, number and nature of doors and windows and the design of the rough frames for them. Remember the importance of the highly insulated "thermal envelope" in your superinsulation strategy. One of your structure's biggest "nosebleeds", energy-wise, will be the doors and windows. Despite extensive Research & Development, the R-value of even the most expensive doors and windows does not begin to approach that of a bale wall. Even so, it does make long-term sense to purchase units that provide double or triple the R-value of the low-cost units. For valuable counsel, consult Carmody et al. (1996). Don't be penny-wise, (energy) dollar foolish when you shop for doors and windows!

Using the model (or if you didn't build one, the scaled drawings that you made of the bale layouts for the first and second courses), you can now proceed to prepare a scaled vertical wall-map (i.e., an "elevation") of each wall, showing the placement of each bale and half bale, all frames (for doors, windows, evaporative coolers, etc.) and lintels (if any), as viewed <u>from the outside</u> (don't ever stand inside the building when using one of these maps to position a niche or opening). These maps are invaluable during the wall-raising and should be posted in front of each wall for frequent, convenient reference.

• **Create, or have someone create for you, a complete set of working drawings.** Before moving on to creating your final working drawings, review all decisions about foundation, RBA and roof design, and plumbing, mechanical, and electrical systems. This will ensure that any changes made along the way are still accommodated by the floor plan and that the choices you have made about separate things at different times have not created conflict or redundancy. Do a reality check for things that are easy to draw, but no fun to do, perhaps repeatedly.

Now prepare, or have prepared for you (by an architect or construction draftsperson), detailed, scaled working drawings. They will provide with words and lines a record of the multitude of design decisions you have made. Even years later, a good set of plans will make clear what you decided, and wanted to do, years earlier. We recommend that you have, as a minimum, the following:

• A site plan, showing how the building fits on the site, along with any easements, power sources, underground pipes, etc.

• A floor plan, showing interior partitions, window and door openings, stairways, porch extensions, etc.

• A foundation plan, showing locations of foundation bolts, rebar "imbalers", eyebolts, tubing for threading tie-down straps, etc.

• A cross-section of the foundation system, showing reinforcement bars (a.k.a. "rebar"), perimeter insulation, floor design, etc.

• A roof-framing plan.

• Cross-sections of the wall system itself, and at typical doors and windows

• "Elevations" of each wall, plus detailed sketches of each door and window frame.

• A plumbing and mechanical plan.

• An electrical plan.

These same drawings will constitute much of the package that you will have to provide if you are applying for a building permit. Consult with your local building officials regarding their specific plan requirements for a permit application. Useful resources for this process include Weidhaas (1989), Spence (1993), and Curran (1995).

Having lead you by the nose through this whole confusing, joyful, messy, challenging frustrating process, we'd like to break it to you gently that there is another way to more rapidly, and (perhaps) less expensively, end up with a set of working drawings. Unless you are firmly committed to having a custom, one-of-a-kind design, you may want to explore buying an "off the shelf" plan set. By selling the same design to several parties, the designer can sell each set at a reduced price. At least three sources now exist for this type of straw-bale house-plan sets, and more will undoubtedly appear (see Lanning 1995; or contact *Sustainable Support Systems*, [Box 318, Bisbee, AZ, 85603] for information on designs by Steve Kemble, engineer and longtime straw-bale builder; or contact the *Community Eco-Design Network* [Oak Park Neighborhood Center, 1701 Oak Park Ave., N., Minneapolis, MN, 55411] about their planbook).

With a set of working drawings and, perhaps a permit, you are now virtually ready to start building. Up to this point, we've been assuming that you are going to build this house yourself. You may be assuming that, too. Owner-building can be spiritual, joyful, educational, inspiring, economically beneficial, and more. We encourage you to seriously explore the possibility of doing it all yourself. We also encourage you to be realistic about the skills, time, energy, patience, stamina, and perseverance needed for owner building.

If you choose not to try to do it all, consider getting a builder that will let you (and friends/family) help whenever your skills and schedule permit. Or, consider being your own contractor, choosing sub-contractors to do some or all of the work. This does require time (e.g., to educate yourself; to spend the necessary time on the job site), patience (e.g., to negotiate clearly-worded, enforceable contracts), and certain other skills, but can reduce the contractor-built cost by twenty-five to thirty percent. Among the many resources for the owner-contractor are Kilpatrick (1989), Hamilton and Hamilton (1991), Whitten (1991), Shephard (1992), and Heldman (1996). In some cases, hiring a contractor to do the building may be the correct choice. Even then, seriously consider doing the wall-raising as a "community event". The loving energy of your friends and neighbors will infuse the walls, and you will truly own your home in a way that money can't buy.

Preparing a Materials List

At this point, many builders do a "takeoff". In other words, they prepare a comprehensive list of needed materials, doors and windows, hardware, fasteners, etc. (see Alfano 1985, Householder 1992). To prepare such a list, sit down with your plans and a detail-compulsive friend and start with the very first step (usually, building layout). Step through the whole project, one task at a time, and figure out everything you need to buy, borrow, rent, harvest, dig or scavenge to support each task.

Now, review your shopping list. Well in advance of when you will need them on the building site, order any materials not locally available, right off the shelf. Prepare, as

necessary, to store these and other materials on site with whatever protection they require.

Safe and Sensible Bale Storage

The mere fact we give this whole section a *red flag* should tell you that this is serious business. We've never been able to understand why a person would choose to devote the considerable amount of time, energy, money, brain cells, antacids etc. that it takes to get ready to build a straw-bale house, and then not adequately protect the single, most important material they'll be using— THE BALES. And yet, time and again, people let their precious bales become, and stay, wet enough to be rendered useless or suspect.

With the intention of reinforcing your commitment to follow through on this important task, here is what we think constitutes proper storage:

• **Get the bottom course of bales up off the ground**. In many areas, slightly damaged, wooden, loading/shipping pallets are free for the taking and great for this purpose. In any case, find some way to elevate the bottom course of bales.

• **Create a stack that has a curved (a.k.a. crowned) top.** This prevents ponding and gets water off the stack quickly.

• **Protect at least the top of the stack with some sort of waterproof covering that will not be blown off.** One effective system involves first installing a piece of plastic sheeting, large enough to come down a foot or so onto the sides of the stack, where it is fastened with "Roberta Pins" (see page 92) to prevent it from shifting around. This first layer is then protected from sunlight by a canvas or woven polyester tarp, itself tied or weighted down. Silver-colored tarps that are somewhat longer-lasting (i.e., more resistant to ultraviolet light) are available from many suppliers (e.g., *Northern*, 800-535-5545).

Ideally, the edges of the tarp are somehow held slightly out from the sides of the stack, creating a drip edge. See the diagram below for one option. In extremely wet climates, especially if wind-driven rain is common, the sides of the stack may need to wrapped before the top is covered. In this case, be sure that the top edge of the side-wrapping is sufficiently overlapped, on the outside, by the upper covering. A breathable housewrap material would be ideal as a side-wrap.

Here's a final note on storage that relates not to water, but to the length of time the bales have been stored. The longer the storage, the greater the mouse population. This means visible effects of tunneling and the likelihood that they'll chew through an occasional string in the process (not so with wire-tied bales—two more reasons to minimize the time gap between the availability of the year's new batch of bales and the date of your wall-raising.

Whew!

At long last, you should be able to send out invitations for your wall-raising and to tentatively schedule the other activities in the sequence that will lead to a finished building. Veteran builders factor in Murphy's Law, delays in the arrival of materials, bad weather, that unannounced three-week visit by your in-laws, the flu, etc. For each major work effort, list out the people and equipment that you'll need, and figure out how you're going to get them. Don't schedule move-in or the housewarming party quite yet. You'll have plenty of time to do this later as light begins to appear at the end of the tunnel.

And now, into the breach we go!

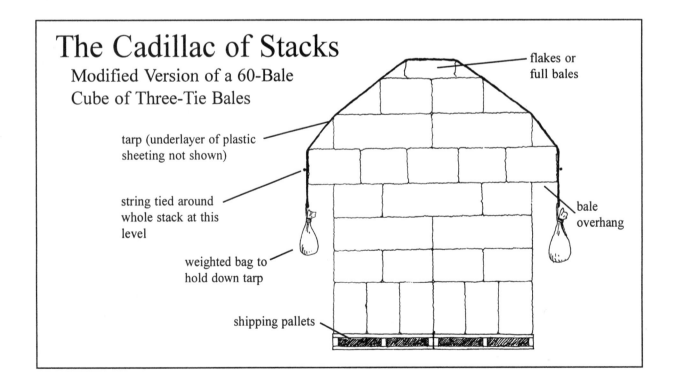

The Cadillac of Stacks
Modified Version of a 60-Bale
Cube of Three-Tie Bales

flakes or full bales

tarp (underlayer of plastic sheeting not shown)

string tied around whole stack at this level

weighted bag to hold down tarp

bale overhang

shipping pallets

Part
Two
Building At Last!

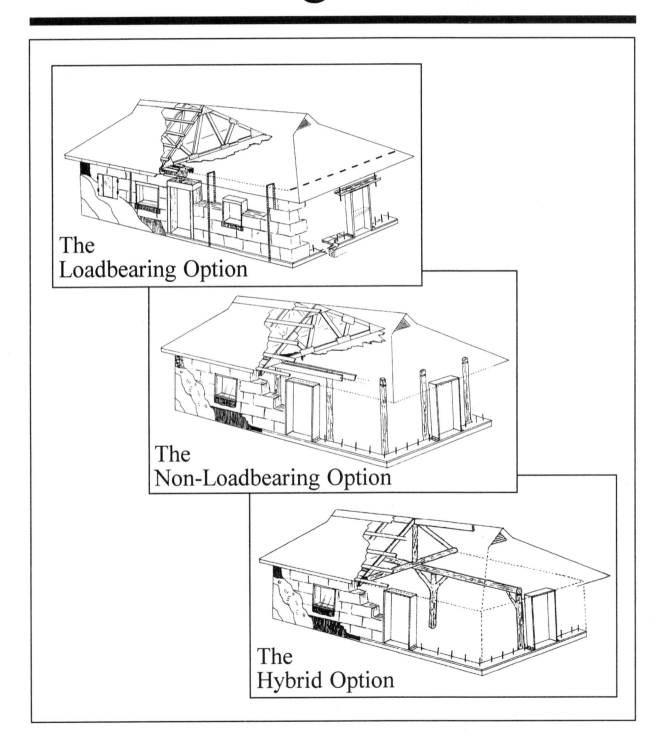

The
Loadbearing Option

The
Non-Loadbearing Option

The
Hybrid Option

The Loadbearing Option

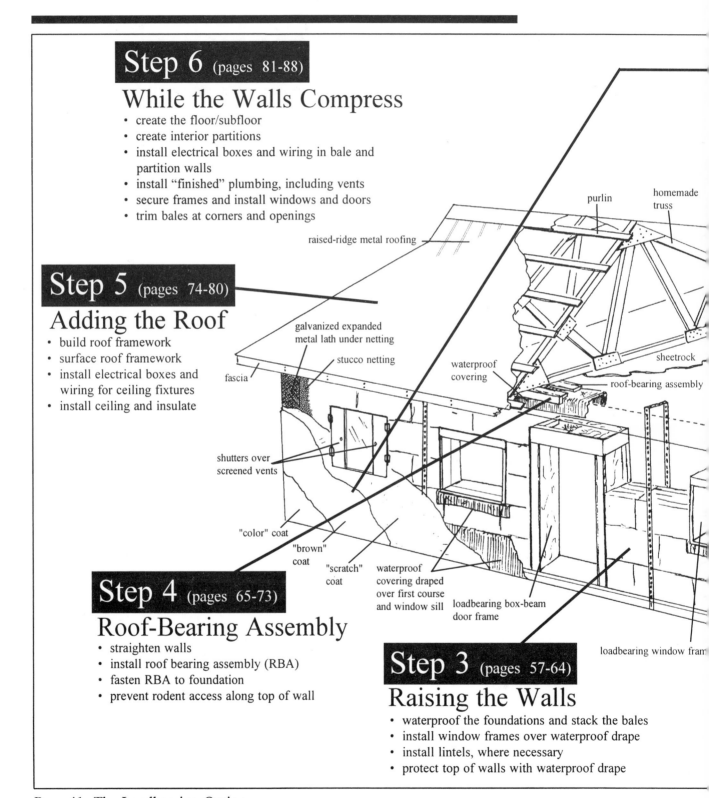

Step 6 (pages 81-88)
While the Walls Compress
- create the floor/subfloor
- create interior partitions
- install electrical boxes and wiring in bale and partition walls
- install "finished" plumbing, including vents
- secure frames and install windows and doors
- trim bales at corners and openings

Step 5 (pages 74-80)
Adding the Roof
- build roof framework
- surface roof framework
- install electrical boxes and wiring for ceiling fixtures
- install ceiling and insulate

Step 4 (pages 65-73)
Roof-Bearing Assembly
- straighten walls
- install roof bearing assembly (RBA)
- fasten RBA to foundation
- prevent rodent access along top of wall

Step 3 (pages 57-64)
Raising the Walls
- waterproof the foundations and stack the bales
- install window frames over waterproof drape
- install lintels, where necessary
- protect top of walls with waterproof drape

purlin

homemade truss

raised-ridge metal roofing

galvanized expanded metal lath under netting

stucco netting

waterproof covering

sheetrock

roof-bearing assembly

fascia

shutters over screened vents

"color" coat

"brown" coat

"scratch" coat

waterproof covering draped over first course and window sill

loadbearing box-beam door frame

loadbearing window fram

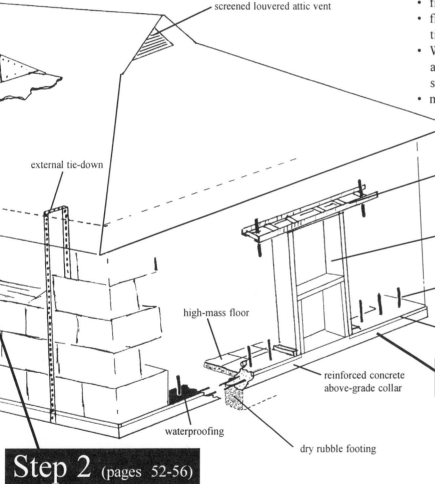

Step 7 (pages 89-117)
Surfacing the Walls
- install expanded metal lath inside and out
- install stucco netting on outside
- plaster the outside wall surfaces
- cover the interior bale surfaces with earthen (a.k.a. mud or adobe) plaster

Step 8 (pages 118-122)
The Finishing Touches
- finish electrical and plumbing details
- finish carpentry details inside and out
- finish preparation for painting, staining, tiling, etc.
- With safety foremost, install roof jack and stovepipe for backup heating system
- make the house a home

screened louvered attic vent

external tie-down

angle-iron lintel

non-loadbearing window frame (convertible to door frame) with gap under lintel

rebar stubs ("imbalers")

pressure-treated wood nailer strip

high-mass floor

reinforced concrete above-grade collar

waterproofing

dry rubble footing

Step 1 (pages 43-51)
Layout and Foundations
- establish corner locations
- erect batter boards and string lines
- install "rough" plumbing and electrical
- create the foundation for the bale walls with appropriate "hardware" in place

Step 2 (pages 52-56)
Window and Door Frames
- fabricate all frames
- attach door frames to foundation

Step 1. Foundations

Challenge: to create a stable, durable base that will minimize the likelihood of water reaching the bales from below and of stress being put on the wall-surfacing materials.

Walk-Through ♟ *

• *During the process of finalizing your design, you will have selected a particular foundation system. Your choice would have been influenced by many factors, perhaps including:*
—*any unusual conditions you encountered during site preparation (e.g., shallow bedrock);*
—*soil testing, re: bearing capacities, expansive clays etc.;*
—*the seismic zone within which you are building;*
—*the total load created by the proposed structure and whether that load is distributed evenly along a wall or is concentrated at certain points;*
—*the depth to the frost line or to permafrost;*
—*and, the relative availability of money vs. owner/ volunteer labor and gatherable materials.*

♣ *Having done the site preparation prior to finalizing the design and getting the final drawings prepared, we can now orient the building shape on the site, giving consideration to passive/solar strategies and other concerns.*

♣ *Stake corner positions using 3-4-5 squaring technique or equivalent. Create batter board system, fine tuning for square and level.*

♣ *Mark ground with lime or equivalent to guide excavations. Remove strings and excavate.*

♣ *Fill trenches to the surface with uniform "rubble" material. Compact as needed.*

♣ *Re-install strings. Create level "forms" to contain the poured concrete, giving consideration to rebar placement, waterproof perimeter insulation board, stucco netting attachment, plumbing and other passageways. Wood used to build your forms can be more easily used later (e.g., for framed partition walls) if kept clean during the pour. Kraft paper, plastic sheeting, etc., stapled to "at risk" surfaces, will save you much cleanup time later.*

• *Wet, pourable concrete is very heavy, and while still fluid, exerts pressure against the forms. The deeper the concrete, the greater the outward pressure. Poorly braced and/or cross-tied forms can "blow out"; at best, you get unwanted bulges; at worst, concrete gets wasted and the forms have to be rebuilt. Extra bracing and cross-ties are cheap insurance.*

♣ *Mix, pour, settle and screed concrete, placing any hardware (e.g., "imbalers", foundation bolts, eyebolts) before it becomes too stiff. The "imbalers" are typically 18 inch [46 cm] long, straight pieces of 1/2 inch [1.3 cm] diameter reinforcing bar [a.k.a. rebar]. About 6 inches [15.2 cm] are in the concrete, leaving about 12 inches [30.5 cm] sticking up to "imbale" the first course of bales, the purpose being to prevent them from being accidentally bumped out of their desired position. For an expensive but non-metallic, alternative, try fiberglass rebar.*

If possible, place no foundation bolt (for threaded rod tie-downs) closer than 1-1/4 bale lengths from a corner so all corner bales can be placed and adjusted without hassle. For tie-downs closer than 1-1/4 bale lengths, use an external system.

♣ *You'll play hell getting something into concrete or making a hole through concrete once it has set up (i.e., become rocklike). To*

---

* You may want to re-read the section on "How This Guide Is Organized" (page 2) before plunging ahead.   There is a method to the madness.

help you remember to place, and to position accurately, all the hardware, use your detailed, scaled, foundation drawing (the plan, or "from above", view), as a guide. Measure carefully and mark on the forms where every item of hardware is to go and as soon as they are in, use the drawing to double check.

♣ *Trowel the area the bales will sit on to a flat, relatively smooth surface, then keep moist for a maximum-strength cure. Any concrete that will remain exposed should be troweled to the desired finish at this time.*

♣ *To provide protection against the sharp edge left by the rebar cutter at the top end of the imbalers, you may want to temporarily cover them with plastic jugs, beverage cans, "dead" tennis balls or the like.*

♣ *After removing the formwork, modify the ground surface to assure good drainage away from the foundation.*

Dimensioning Your Foundation

As discussed earlier under *Finalizing Your Design*, most builders choose not to use foundation dimensions that are arbitrary or based on some non-bale-related module. They do this to avoid having to create many custom-length bales in each course and to avoid having these shortened bales break up the "running bond" (where each bale overlaps the two bales below it by nearly equal amounts).

The preferred approach is to let the chosen bale layout for the first course and the "effective bale length" (see page 35) dictate the length and width measurements for whatever platform the bales will sit on. It's better to have this "foundation" slightly oversized in terms of the length dimensions, since stuffing loose "flakes" of straw into occasional small gaps is much easier than retying bales to

shorten them. Since the "effective bale length" of typical 3-tie bales is close to, but very seldom greater than 48 inches [1.22 m], many builders use this as a standard module for calculating the exact dimensions of their foundation. Based on the width of the actual bales you use, the width of any concrete collar or "toe-up" platform will be about 18 in. [45.7 cm] for 2-tie bales and about 23 in. [58.4 cm] for 3-tie bales, including the width of any waterproof perimeter insulation, assuming that the bales are laid "flat".

Building Layout

The purpose of layout is to accurately establish the location of the corners of the outside edge of the element (e.g., slab, grade beam, wooden deck) on which the bottom course of bales will rest (see diagram next page).

The use of batter boards and string lines enables the builder to reestablish these corner points even though corner pins initially placed in the ground have been disturbed or removed. By positioning the horizontal cross-members of the batter boards at the same elevation (using, for example, a commercial hose level kit and a carpenter's level), the strings can then also be used as a "bench mark" from which one can measure down to establish the correct depth of a trench or the correct height of formwork for containing poured concrete. Since small errors can be cumulative during the building process, it make sense to insure that the layout accurately reflects the dimensions and shape shown on your final drawings. However, most straw-bale builders feel comfortable with diagonals (corner-to-corner measurements) that differ by as much as a half inch.

References we can recommend for building layout are Jackson (1979) and Law (1982b).

Concrete

Concrete is a chemically-hardened mixture of cement, sand, gravel and water. A

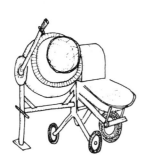

standard mixture is 1 part (by volume) Portland cement, 2 parts sand, and 3 parts gravel.

Make sure that your forming system is level and strong enough to withstand the very considerable outward (and to a lesser extent upward) pressure that will be put on it by the wet concrete. Make sure that any passages through the concrete that will be required for later installation of pipes or electrical wires have been accounted for. Mark your formwork with some easily visible code system that shows where various items of hardware (e.g., rebar stubs, eye-bolts, foundation bolts) need to be inserted into the still-wet concrete.

If using site-mixed concrete, consider equipment, labor and time requirements and local availability of acceptable sand and gravel. If using truck-delivered, already-mixed concrete, consider access for the truck and its chute, helpers and equipment needed to handle a large amount of concrete in a short time. For additional tips, consult Kern (1975), Syvanen (1983), MWPS (1989b) or Loy (1990).

Calculate the cubic yards of concrete needed by multiplying the length by the width by the height of the foundation and/or slab (in feet), then dividing by 27 (the number of cubic feet in a cubic yard). Add 10% to the calculated amount to ensure having enough, and prepare a place to beneficially use any excess.

Building Layout

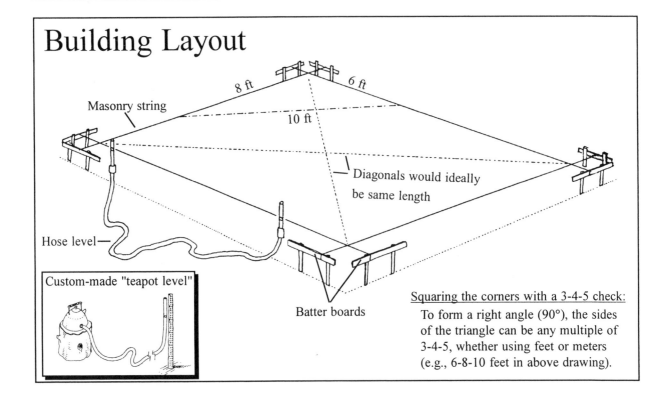

Masonry string

8 ft   6 ft

10 ft

Diagonals would ideally be same length

Hose level

Custom-made "teapot level"

Batter boards

Squaring the corners with a 3-4-5 check:
To form a right angle (90°), the sides of the triangle can be any multiple of 3-4-5, whether using feet or meters (e.g., 6-8-10 feet in above drawing).

Forming Your Foundation

Wooden (pressure-treated preferred) nailer strip temporarily attached to the framework (and backed with spikes for firm connection to concrete) for fastening stucco netting and any waterproof drape. Other fastening options shown below.

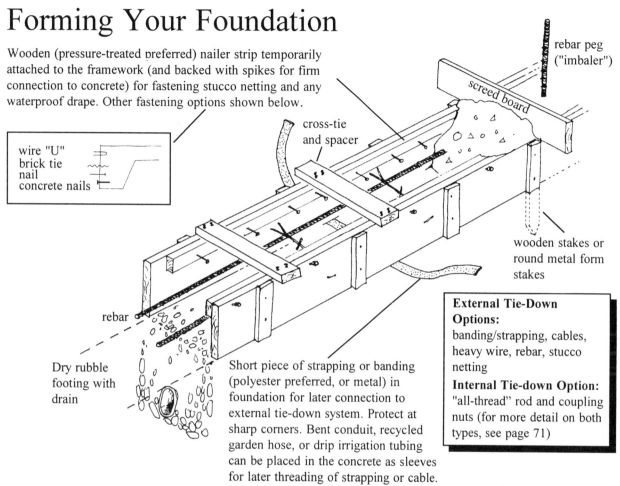

wire "U"
brick tie
nail
concrete nails

rebar peg ("imbaler")

screed board

cross-tie and spacer

wooden stakes or round metal form stakes

rebar

Dry rubble footing with drain

Short piece of strapping or banding (polyester preferred, or metal) in foundation for later connection to external tie-down system. Protect at sharp corners. Bent conduit, recycled garden hose, or drip irrigation tubing can be placed in the concrete as sleeves for later threading of strapping or cable.

External Tie-Down Options: banding/strapping, cables, heavy wire, rebar, stucco netting

Internal Tie-down Option: "all-thread" rod and coupling nuts (for more detail on both types, see page 71)

Forming a One-step, Toed-up, Monolithic Foundation and Slab

eyebolts (typical) for external tie-down of roof bearing assembly

For information on pouring this type of foundation/slab over bales to provide below-slab insulation, see page 88.

form stake must be pulled out as soon as the concrete sets up sufficiently

Forming a Two-step, Toed-up Foundation and Slab with Bales

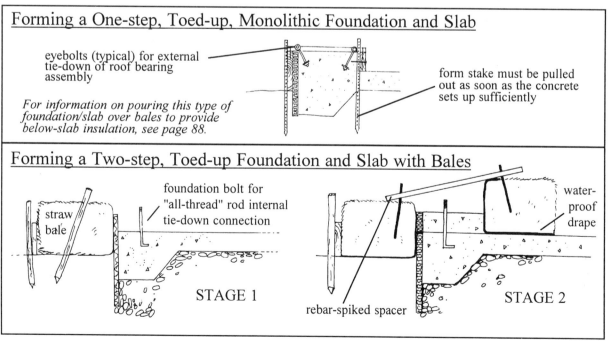

straw bale

foundation bolt for "all-thread" rod internal tie-down connection

water-proof drape

STAGE 1

rebar-spiked spacer

STAGE 2

The Argument for Toe-ups

Savvy, modern straw-builders have always created foundations that kept the bales at least 6 inches [15.2 cm] above grade (a.k.a. ground level) on the outside, but often had the bales sitting directly on the waterproofed edge of a slab poured simultaneously with the foundation. Considerable experience (sometimes involving serious anxiety and harsh, retrospective self-criticism) suggests that it is also well worth the trouble to elevate the bales at least 1-1/2 to 2 inches above the slab on the inside. One cloudburst before you get the roof on, or a plumbing disaster that floods the floor for days while you're on vacation, would convince you beyond a doubt that you should have provided a toe-up. Trust us, Just do it!

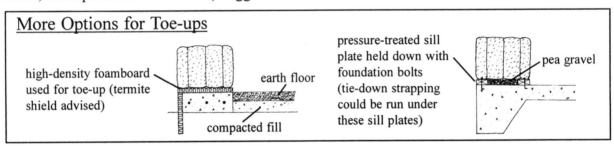

More Options for Toe-ups

high-density foamboard used for toe-up (termite shield advised)

earth floor

compacted fill

pressure-treated sill plate held down with foundation bolts (tie-down strapping could be run under these sill plates)

pea gravel

Perimeter Insulation–Some Considerations

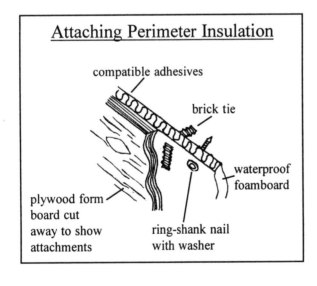

Attaching Perimeter Insulation

compatible adhesives

brick tie

waterproof foamboard

plywood form board cut away to show attachments

ring-shank nail with washer

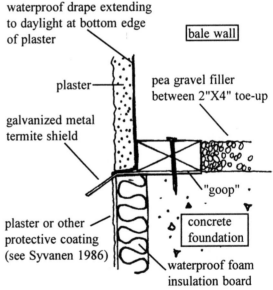

waterproof drape extending to daylight at bottom edge of plaster

bale wall

plaster

galvanized metal termite shield

pea gravel filler between 2"X4" toe-up

"goop"

plaster or other protective coating (see Syvanen 1986)

concrete foundation

waterproof foam insulation board

Perimeter Insulation and Termites

Termites can easily burrow up through foam insulation and bales, gaining access to wooden door and window frames. In areas where termites pose a significant threat, a metal termite shield should be strongly considered. One option for detailing shown above right.

Other Foundation Options

Steeply-Sloped Lots

Sloping building sites present problems to the straw-bale builder. Using the "cut-and-fill" approach may require massive earth moving that results in ugly "cut walls" that need retaining. Step footings have their own problems, especially in load-bearing structures.

A better solution may be to use a grid of vertical columns or posts to support a wooden deck upon which the straw-bale house can sit. In most climates, the underside of this deck will need to be insulated. Possibilities range from batts (e.g., fiberglass, cotton, or cellulose) to straw bales or flakes (see page 88), to using insulative structural floor panels to create the deck. Such panels usually have a foam core, but Agiboard, Inc. is manufacturing in Texas a panel consisting of compressed straw (for insulation), sandwiched between two layers of oriented strand board (for structure). Access: an Iowa telephone number, (515) 472-0363 or e-mail <agriboard@lisco.com>.

The space under the deck can be closed in with (straw-bale?) skirting, and used for storage (this would be a great place for storing water harvested from the roof). See Levin (1991) regarding further options for sloping sites.

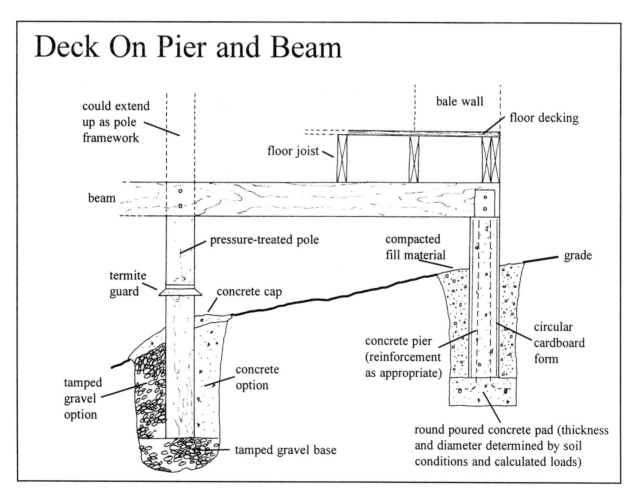

Deck On Pier and Beam

could extend up as pole framework

bale wall

floor decking

floor joist

beam

pressure-treated pole

termite guard

concrete cap

compacted fill material

grade

tamped gravel option

concrete option

concrete pier (reinforcement as appropriate)

circular cardboard form

tamped gravel base

round poured concrete pad (thickness and diameter determined by soil conditions and calculated loads)

Low-Tech Ideas*

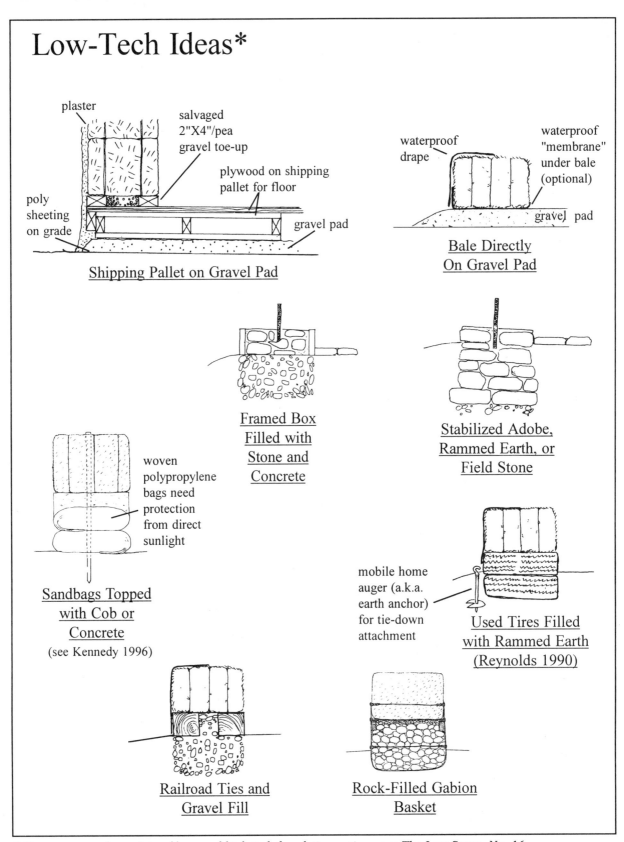

plaster

salvaged 2"X4"/pea gravel toe-up

plywood on shipping pallet for floor

poly sheeting on grade

gravel pad

Shipping Pallet on Gravel Pad

waterproof drape

waterproof "membrane" under bale (optional)

gravel pad

Bale Directly On Gravel Pad

Framed Box Filled with Stone and Concrete

Stabilized Adobe, Rammed Earth, or Field Stone

woven polypropylene bags need protection from direct sunlight

Sandbags Topped with Cob or Concrete

(see Kennedy 1996)

mobile home auger (a.k.a. earth anchor) for tie-down attachment

Used Tires Filled with Rammed Earth (Reynolds 1990)

Railroad Ties and Gravel Fill

Rock-Filled Gabion Basket

For coverage of a variety of low- and high-tech foundation options, see The Last Straw, *No. 16.*

High Tech Idea For Unusual Conditions*

- Want to do slab-on-grade but shallow bedrock makes excavating for a pad and the integral toed-down foundation prohibitively expensive?
- Have soil conditions (e.g., expansive clays) that are likely to cause cracking in an ordinary slab-on-grade?

The answer (maybe): an 8 inch [20.3 cm] thick, post-tensioned "engineered slab" (see diagram below), with a grid of stainless steel cables that are used to put the slab into compression several days after the pour. Not cheap, but may be the least expensive of the few, working options.

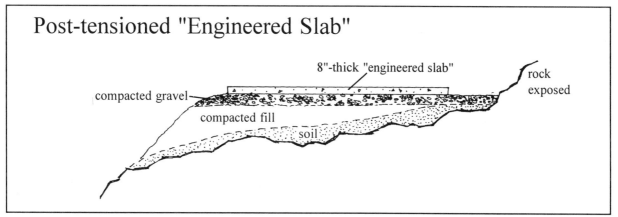

Post-tensioned "Engineered Slab"

8"-thick "engineered slab"

rock exposed

compacted gravel

compacted fill

soil

* Low Tech Idea for Unusual Conditions: accept reality and choose another building site.

Foundation Strategies for Cold Climates

One downside of our inevitably wide bale walls is that any concrete platform on which they rest must also be wide. In areas where freezing temperatures are encountered at considerable depth, it would require large amounts of concrete to create a uniformly-wide concrete footing extending to below this "frost line". The related costs, both financial and environmental, dictate that we explore alternatives.

One possible solution is the "I-beam" concept, suggested to us by architect Arlen Raikes. The "I" cross-section, being narrower in the middle, requires the use of less cement-based materials.

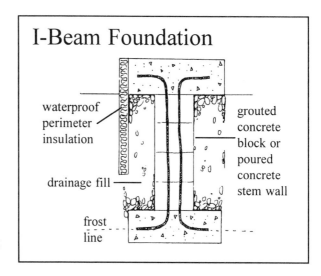

I-Beam Foundation

waterproof perimeter insulation

grouted concrete block or poured concrete stem wall

drainage fill

frost line

Another approach, suggested to Frank Lloyd Wright (see Wright 1954) by Welsh-born masons in Wisconsin, is the "dry wall footing" (a.k.a. dry rubble footing, rubble trench footing). As Wright used this strategy, trenches were dug only sixteen inches deep to contain "rubble", even though the frost line depth was about four feet below ground surface. He assumed that if the material under the above-grade collar (which in his case, at Taliesen, consisted of linear blocks of limestone laid end to end) could be kept dry, there could be no destructive "frost heaving" even if the soil temperature dropped below freezing. The Taliesen experience was not without problems, and modern users have generally chosen, or been required by building officials, to dig the trenches to below the frost line depth. This requires the use of

more "rubble" to fill the trenches to the surface, but "rubble" is less costly to buy and place than concrete. Two useful references on the modern use of this approach are Velonis (1983) and Tom (1996).

The word "rubble", as used in this connection, includes a variety of coarse, quickly-draining materials. Wright used "fist-sized broken rock" in his trenches. Modern builders have used everything from "river run" (rounded pebbles which settle automatically to a stable configuration), to "leach field rock" (angular fragments that should be compacted mechanically).

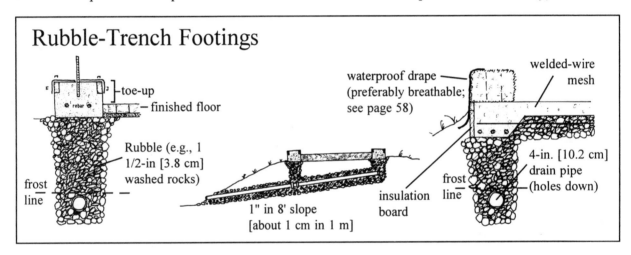

Rubble-Trench Footings

toe-up
rebar
finished floor

Rubble (e.g., 1 1/2-in [3.8 cm] washed rocks)

frost line

1" in 8' slope [about 1 cm in 1 m]

waterproof drape (preferably breathable; see page 58)

insulation board

welded-wire mesh

frost line

4-in. [10.2 cm] drain pipe (holes down)

A third approach (shown below) is the "shallow, frost-protected footing" concept described in a publication prepared by the National Association of Home Builders Research Center for the US Dept. of Housing and Urban Development (HUD 1995). This approach is based on the use of strategically placed waterproof, foam-board perimeter

insulation to modify the frost line surface such that a frost-free zone is created under and around the edges of the building "footprint". This enables the builder to safely position the bottom of the footing well above the "normal" frost line. For an excellent summary, see Malin (1995b).

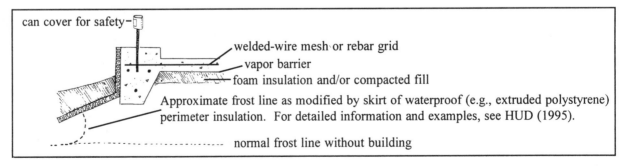

can cover for safety

welded-wire mesh or rebar grid
vapor barrier
foam insulation and/or compacted fill
Approximate frost line as modified by skirt of waterproof (e.g., extruded polystyrene) perimeter insulation. For detailed information and examples, see HUD (1995).

normal frost line without building

Step 2. Door and Window Frames

Challenge: to create, based on the load they will be carrying, frame/lintel combinations to accommodate each door and window. They should carry this load without deforming, while using no more materials than necessary.

Walk-Through

- *The dimensioning and design of the window and door frames should have been done as part of finalizing your design and preparing a set of plans. Several generic approaches to sizing window openings are shown below. All three could be used in the same building.*
- ♣ *Using the information from your plans, fabricate the rough frames in advance of the wall-raising. Use sturdy corner or diagonal braces to keep them square until progress requires their removal.*
- ♣ *Position door and floor-mounted window frames onto the foundation. Once they have been secured, provide temporary bracing to keep them upright and level.*
- ♣ *Fabricate any separate lintels that you will use above non-loadbearing frames. Lintels, generically, are assemblies, located above openings, that carry any load created by materials above those openings.*

Loadbearing versus Non-Loadbearing Walls

Even in a loadbearing design, the roof load (dead and live) is usually carried entirely by two of the walls. For a rectangular building, the **loadbearing** walls are usually the two longer walls

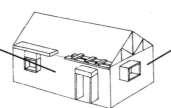

This means that the other two walls are called **non-loadbearing walls**, since they carry no roof load. Frames or lintels in these walls are thus carrying only the weight of any bales located above these openings.

Sizing Openings

1. Modify bales to fit around the rough frames built for arbitrarily positioned, standard windows or pre-hung doors.
2. Make frames to fit openings dictated by the one-half bale module and the bale height module. Doors and windows will probably have to be custom made if the full opening is to be used.

3. As in # 2, make frames to fit the bale-modular opening. Then, make a second, perhaps lighter, internal frame to fit a standard window or pre-hung door. The space difference between the smaller internal frame and the larger bale-modular opening can be used to create angled openings on the interior or exterior. See the diagram on page 56 (middle right) for details.

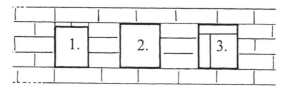

Lintel Options

Integral Option

In this option, the upper member of the frame is a built-in (a.k.a. integral) lintel, rigid enough to carry the load from above without deforming (bending). This load is transferred by the side members to the foundation (in the case of a door frame), or to the bottom member, which transfers it to the bales below (in the case of a window frame). In terms of compressive load (load from above), the frame replaces the bales left out to create the opening. Therefore, they cause no increase in the load carried by the columns of bales on either side of the opening. This option is illustrated on page 55, lower left.

Separate Option

Separate lintels are not part of the frame. They extend out on to the bale walls and transfer the load from above, onto the bales on either side of the opening. They can be located at the top of the wall, as in the case where a rigid roof bearing assembly (RBA) acts also as a lintel across openings. They can also be located immediately above the frame, as in the case of an angle-iron lintel (see the diagram for the Non-loadbearing Door Frame and Lintel on page 55, upper right). In such cases, the lintels should extend out onto the walls at least one-half the width of the opening, and no less than 2 feet [61 cm]. They are not commonly used for openings more than 4 feet [1.22 m] wide and are most often used in non-loadbearing walls. Separate lintels always increase the load carried by the bale columns adjacent to the openings they span.

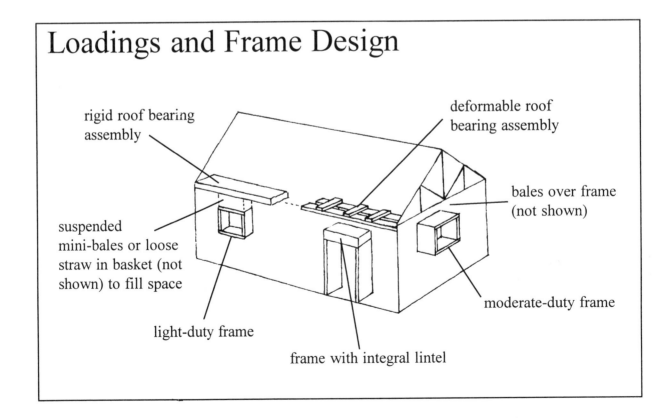

Loadings and Frame Design

rigid roof bearing assembly

deformable roof bearing assembly

bales over frame (not shown)

suspended mini-bales or loose straw in basket (not shown) to fill space

light-duty frame

frame with integral lintel

moderate-duty frame

Selecting Frame/Lintel Combinations for Openings

<u>Axiom</u>: *Each opening has the potential of being a unique case.*

How sturdy a particular frame needs to be will depend primarily on how much compressive load it will carry. This can vary from a lot (imagine a wide opening in a loadbearing wall that is carrying half the weight of a tile-surfaced roof that sits on a non-rigid roof bearing assembly) to nothing (imagine a non-loadbearing wall with a modest opening spanned by an angle-iron lintel).

In order to design a frame that can carry its particular load without deforming, while using no more materials than necessary, this load must be calculated or "guesstimated". Engineers and architects use charts which relate both load and span lengths to deformation. Don't hesitate to use their expertise if you are uneasy about making these decisions yourself, particularly if you want wide openings in loadbearing walls.

Another approach is to assess the factors affecting the load at that opening, make a ballpark estimate of the load situation on a scale from 1 (no load) to 10 (really heavy load), and then err on the side of caution. Many successful, simple, loadbearing structures have been built with frame/lintel systems designed this way by their owner-builders.

A list of factors that can affect the load on a given frame would include:

• the width of the opening;
• whether there will be a separate (non-integral) lintel above the frame;
• the number of courses of bales (if any) there are above the frame;
• the relative rigidity of the roof-bearing assembly (RBA) above the opening;
• whether the opening is in a loadbearing or non-loadbearing wall;
• the distance between the loadbearing walls and the weight per square foot of the roof/ceiling/insulation system;
• the weight of the RBA;
• and, maximum anticipated live load (e.g., snow).

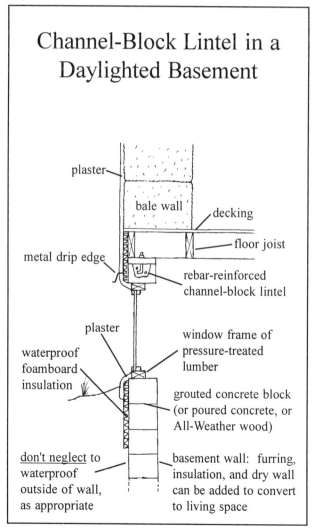

Channel-Block Lintel in a Daylighted Basement

plaster

bale wall

decking

floor joist

metal drip edge

rebar-reinforced channel-block lintel

plaster

window frame of pressure-treated lumber

waterproof foamboard insulation

grouted concrete block (or poured concrete, or All-Weather wood)

<u>don't neglect</u> to waterproof outside of wall, as appropriate

basement wall: furring, insulation, and dry wall can be added to convert to living space

Loadbearing Options

Box Beam Door Frame

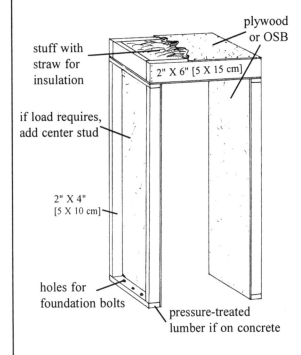

stuff with straw for insulation

plywood or OSB

2" X 6" [5 X 15 cm]

if load requires, add center stud

2" X 4" [5 X 10 cm]

holes for foundation bolts

pressure-treated lumber if on concrete

Window Frame with Integral Box Beam Lintel and Bottom

Nominal 2 inch [5 cm] thick lumber. For wider openings (i.e., greater loads) you may also want to use the box beam approach for the sides, as well.

Non-Loadbearing Options

Non-Loadbearing Door Frame and Lintel

typical 2" X 2" X 3/16" [5 X 5 X 0.5 cm] angle iron; metal straps 2" X 3/16" [5 X 0.5 cm]

angle-iron lintel

12" [30 cm] rebar peg above and below

overhang = 1/2 the width of opening with 24" [61 cm] minimum

leave gap to accomodate settling

expanded metal lath

2" X 10-12" [5 X 25-30 cm]

Option: 2" X 4" [5 X 10 cm] bolted to foundation

Option: metal bracket/angle-iron

Concrete, above-ground collar as toe-up

RBA As Lintel

rigid wooden RBA (or concrete bond beam) can act as lintel

space under rigid RBA insulated with loose straw in expanded metal lath "basket" (not shown)

angle-iron attached to both sides of less-rigid RBA over openings

Some Details for Frames

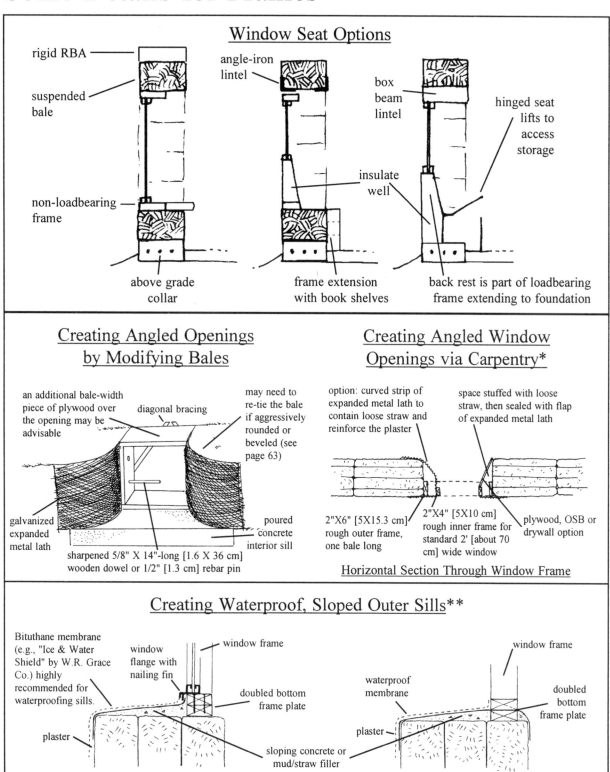

Window Seat Options

rigid RBA

suspended bale

non-loadbearing frame

above grade collar

angle-iron lintel

insulate well

frame extension with book shelves

box beam lintel

hinged seat lifts to access storage

back rest is part of loadbearing frame extending to foundation

Creating Angled Openings by Modifying Bales

an additional bale-width piece of plywood over the opening may be advisable

diagonal bracing

may need to re-tie the bale if aggressively rounded or beveled (see page 63)

galvanized expanded metal lath

poured concrete interior sill

sharpened 5/8" X 14"-long [1.6 X 36 cm] wooden dowel or 1/2" [1.3 cm] rebar pin

Creating Angled Window Openings via Carpentry*

option: curved strip of expanded metal lath to contain loose straw and reinforce the plaster

space stuffed with loose straw, then sealed with flap of expanded metal lath

2"X6" [5X15.3 cm] rough outer frame, one bale long

2"X4" [5X10 cm] rough inner frame for standard 2' [about 70 cm] wide window

plywood, OSB or drywall option

Horizontal Section Through Window Frame

Creating Waterproof, Sloped Outer Sills**

Bituthane membrane (e.g., "Ice & Water Shield" by W.R. Grace Co.) highly recommended for waterproofing sills.

window flange with nailing fin

window frame

doubled bottom frame plate

plaster

sloping concrete or mud/straw filler

waterproof membrane

plaster

window frame

doubled bottom frame plate

*See page 128 for same frame design, different use. ** See also page 59.*

Step 3. Raising the Walls

Challenge: to create sound walls that match your expectations for function and form, in a way that reflects your interest in human interaction.

Walk-Through

• *Have all your building materials, hardware, and tools assembled on the site, along with a First Aid Kit and dust masks for your workers. You should also have on hand brooms, rakes and a supply of large, sturdy garbage bags for storing the loose straw that you will periodically want to gather and remove from the working area.* **Loose straw is a major fire hazard.** *Keeping the site cleaned up will greatly reduce the risk of fire, will make the site safer for the workers and will reduce the likelihood that small (but very necessary) tools will disappear when laid on the ground (a bad idea in any case). Cleanup provides an ideal opportunity for even very young and very old volunteers to get meaningfully involved in the excitement. The bagged, loose straw comes in handy for filling cracks and stuffing openings as you build. Also, mixed with a clay-rich soil and water, it can be used to put a fireproof cap over the stuffed openings. Any that still remains will make great mulch for your organic garden. If the weather permits, uncover your bale-storage stacks to give them a final chance to become fully dry.*

♣ *You need to ensure that the bales will not be resting on a surface that becomes moist from water moving up from below. You can do this by having them rest on a material that will not "wick" water upward (e.g., pea gravel) or by sealing the surface they rest on with a waterproofing "membrane" (e.g., roofing felt, plastic sheeting, various asphalt-based compounds, or combinations*

thereof). Be careful to seal around the protruding rebar stubs ("imbalers") and any foundation bolts. As desired—or as required—install a termite barrier (e.g., galvanized sheet metal, appropriately bent).

♣ *Install* <u>sturdy</u>, *temporary corner guides, as desired. These help keep the corners vertical and, with string lines pulled between them, can help you keep your walls (especially long ones) straight and vertical. When a corner guide gets knocked out of "plumb" (i.e., out of a vertical position), it becomes your enemy. It gives the false impression that the corner is still going up vertically, although it is not.* **Attach your corner guides very securely and check them often for plumb.** *Where two walls meet at a corner that is out of plumb, verticality can be achieved only by dismantling and rebuilding it.*

A building with only curved walls will have no place for corner guides, but similar guides can be erected to ensure that the walls go up vertically. You'll get smoother surfaces if you bend the bales.

• *If a large number of people will be assisting, it will help to break them up into working teams. These can consist of an experienced "wall captain" (for ongoing problem spotting and quality control) and four or five inexperienced members (for bale inspection, carrying, placing and pinning). It also helps to have a several two-person crews set up to make half- and custom-length bales. Be sure to have at least one bale needle for each crew (better yet, two).*

Encourage people to trade jobs occasionally.

• *If you have chosen to have your wall-raising be a "Y'all come!", community-building event, you will probably want to cordon off the work site from the socialization area.*

• *Before any bales are laid, it may be valuable to ask the workers to be mindful of job safety, to review with them the "rules of thumb" for laying bales (see page 63), and to inoculate them against the insidious "bale-laying frenzy".*

*If you'll be having a lot of enthusiastic, but inexperienced, people help with the bale-stacking, you might want to **get the first course of bales in place the previous day**. You'll want the first course "imbaled" such that they are properly lined up relative to the edges of the toe-up. This can be time-consuming and takes care and patience (the opposite of enthusiastic "bale frenzy"). The pre-positioning of the first-course bales also provides a pattern for the volunteers as they start the second course and hides the "imbalers" where people can't trip over them.*

♣ *Start laying bales at corners and on both sides of door frames, lining them up accurately with the edge of the "foundation". At the door (and later, the window) frames, many builders leave a gap of about one-half inch [1.25 cm.] between the frame and the adjacent bales. This prevents the compressing bale walls from exerting enough pressure on the frames to deform them. A narrower gap will suffice in non-loadbearing walls.*

• *If an internal RBA tie-down system is being used, some bales will have to be lowered down over all-thread rods. With practice, and careful measuring and marking of the "insertion spot" on the bottom of the bale, one can generally get the bale to the desired location on the first try.*

• *Before starting the second course, many builders put in place a waterproof drape. In some jurisdictions, code requires it. This drape should start about six inches [15.2 cm] in from the outside top edge of the bales and then extend down over the outside surface and down past the top of the foundation for several inches. Breathable (i.e., vapor permeable) "house wrap" products are a logical choice (in very wet climates, consider using Tyvek Stucco-Wrap). They conform easily to the irregular wall surfaces, they are tear/puncture resistant, and they are designed to keep liquid water (from rain or snow) out, while still allowing water vapor present in the bales to move toward the outside. The bales in the second course are offset from the pattern set by the first course of bales, overlapping them in order to form a "running bond".*

♣ *You can increase the stability at corners by driving in one or two "staples", bent from short lengths of rebar, where the corner-forming bales butt in each course (see the large drawing on page 61). They can also be used in situations where additional connection between bales is desired (e.g., above a lintel). An alternative is shown below.*

With help of needle tool, tie corner bales together with twine or baling wire

• *The last few bales that will complete a section of wall should be put in place temporarily so that you can measure the size of the gap, if any, or any overlap. If the gap or overlap is very small, you may be able to find and substitute longer or shorter bales. Otherwise, fill the gap (make into two gaps if larger than about 4 inches [1.2 cm]) with a "flake" from a "bad" bale, or adjust for the* overlap by shortening a bale.

• *If corner guides are not being used, make diligent use of a carpenter's level (attached to the edge of a straight board) to maintain verticality at the corners, the only part of the walls impossible to mechanically "tweak" (i.e., bash, pound, or push into place) after they are finished. Since corners typically end up sloping slightly outward, some builders try to slope the tops of the walls slightly inward at the corners to compensate for this phenomenon.*

RED

• ***Temporarily brace any long, tall walls, especially in windy regions.*** *One simple and effective system for bracing such walls is shown below.*

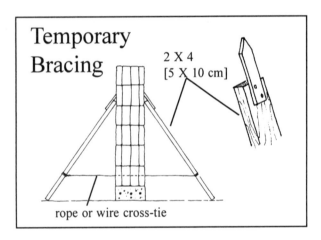

Temporary Bracing

2 X 4
[5 X 10 cm]

rope or wire cross-tie

• *If your design includes long, and/or tall walls, you may also want to incorporate one or more horizontal or vertical elements to stiffen or buttress them. To be effective in a loadbearing wall, horizontal elements must span the entire distance between adjacent, right-angle, buttressing walls and be firmly attached to them. Since such elements are more commonly used in non-loadbearing designs, we have provided more detailed information in* Step 5 *of the* Non-Loadbearing Option.

♣ *The door frames will have been fastened to the foundation before any bales are laid, but window frames, except in the rare case where they will sit on the foundation, cannot be set in place until the proper wall height is reached. After a waterproof covering has been placed over the wall at the correct location along the length of the wall, the frame can be positioned within the wall width as previously determined. Many choose to maximize the interior sill-shelf, and minimize potential water damage, by mounting the windows essentially flush to the outside surface. An exception might be south-facing windows, in a design without roof overhangs, where small windows can be shaded from summer sun by placement to the inside, above a well-sloped and well-waterproofed exterior sill (see the bottom diagram on page 56). Whatever placement is chosen, the frames should then be braced as needed to keep them safely upright. Using a bubble level, check the bottom, horizontal member of each frame to ensure that it is level and stays that way as the wall goes up. Shim under it as needed.*

• ***It's surprisingly easy, if bale frenzy creeps in, to forget to put in a window frame at the right time and/or place.*** *To avoid such embarrassing lapses of attention, post enlarged versions of your wall maps (see page 36, bottom right) in front of each wall, outside the building. One easy option for posting is to stack several bales, put the map on this "table", and cover it with a piece of transparent plastic held down with Roberta Pins (see page 92).*

RED

All members of the wall team, but especially the wall captain, should familiarize themselves with the map of their wall and should refer to it repeatedly. If, however, you still leave out or incorrectly place a frame, the damage can be easily repaired if you catch the error before the roof-bearing assembly (RBA) is on the walls. You just pull out pins and remove bales as necessary, put the waterproof covering in place, install the frame on it and rebuild the wall. It is possible to retrofit small windows into completed walls, even after they have been surfaced, but it's a lot easier to get them in as the wall goes up.

• If _aggressively_ angled or rounded bales are to be used to widen the interior wall opening at doors or windows, they should be customized and placed on either side of the frames as the wall goes up. _Minor_ rounding can be done after the walls are up. An alternative is to make the frame wider than the door or window and use carpentry to create the bevel on the sides of the opening (see the diagram on page 56).

♣ Bale pinning normally takes place as the walls are being raised, often starting at the fourth course. At window locations, short pins can be driven into the bales beneath the frame, either before or after it is placed on the wall.

It might seem rational to pound the pins in until they are out of sight, since this would ensure that no one could trip over them. Experience suggests that this technique has the major disadvantage that you then can't easily tell where you have already pinned. So, we recommend leaving them just barely visible—no tripping, no frustrating searches!

Rebar pins can account for a large percentage of the total embodied energy* in the wall, reducing the overall "sustainability" of the design. Consider using bamboo or willow!

• Above _non-loadbearing_ frames, some kind of lintel will be needed to bridge across the opening. It distributes the roof and/or wall weight, resulting from materials above the opening, to the bale walls on either side. A generally accepted "rule of thumb" for lintels placed just above a frame in loadbearing

walls is that the lintels should extend out onto the walls on both sides for a distance equal to at least half the width of the opening. Increase this distance if the bales at the opening are significantly rounded or angled. Use of the RBA as a lintel over openings is covered in Step 4.

• Every few courses, check for level and shim with loose straw if necessary. After each course, stuff gaps and depressions with loose straw. Do _not_ force straw into gaps, as that can push a corner bale out of position.

• When the walls have been raised to the desired height, a waterproof covering should be placed along their tops to protect them from rain or snow until the roof has been sheathed. Many builders choose to leave this "cap" in place under the RBA to protect the top of the walls against eventual roof leakage.

With all the bales in place, now is a good time to mechanically "tweak" (e.g., beat, bash, ram, brace) the walls until they are acceptably smooth (i.e., planar) and vertical. If you tend to be compulsive about such things, remember that part of the charm of a straw-bale house can be the "soft irregularity" of the walls.

• Check the walls carefully, inside and out, to make sure that all of the openings are completely stuffed with loose straw. To reduce the risk of fire, some builders go one step further, using a mix of clay-rich soil and straw (use the stuff gathered during your cleanups) to cap all the openings. Should you later surface the walls with a cement-based material, you won't be using an expensive, high-embodied-energy material to fill depressions.

• Finally, if you have chosen to spray the walls with a fire-retardant solution, this is a logical time to do it. For additional information, see page 19.

---

* "Embodied energy" is defined here as the total amount of non-renewable energy used to create a unit weight of a given material.

Customizing Bales

Walls stacked in "running bond" require customized, shorter bales where the walls end against door and window frames. As shown below, first create tight new ties to contain the mini-bales. Then cut the original ties, at the knot, to get the maximum reusable length of twine or wire.

Double-notched Bale Needle
Make from a 36 inch (91.4 cm) piece of (chain-link fence) tension bar or purchase from OOB-By Mail, 1037 E. Linden St., Tucson, AZ 85719.

Diagrams 1 through 6 are views from <u>above</u> of a bale sitting <u>on edge</u>.

1

5

2

6

3

tuck only,
don't tie yet

Diagram 7 is a <u>side view</u> of the bale laying <u>flat</u>

7

4

Pull very tight, clamp at loop with vise-grip pliers (optional) and secure with two "half hitch" knots.

Building the Walls

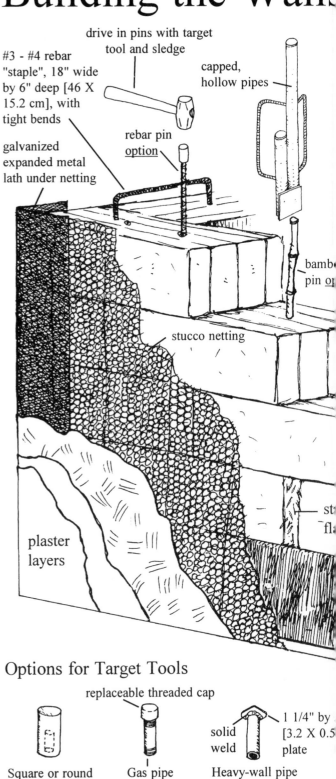

drive in pins with target tool and sledge

#3 - #4 rebar "staple", 18" wide by 6" deep [46 X 15.2 cm], with tight bends

capped, hollow pipes

rebar pin <u>option</u>

galvanized expanded metal lath under netting

bamb
pin o

stucco netting

st
fl

plaster layers

Options for Target Tools

replaceable threaded cap

Square or round steel bar with hole. Lifetime guarantee!

Gas pipe nipple. Least durable.

solid weld

1 1/4" by
[3.2 X 0.5
plate

Heavy-wall pipe (even then, cracks eventually at weld).

Bale Pinning

Popular Pinning System for Loadbearing Designs with 3-Tie Bales Laid Flat

Variations:

1. Short pins, two per bale, penetrating three courses at a time. Start with third course and repeat with all subsequent courses.
2. Eight-ft-long [2.5 m], sharpened "pins" of #5 rebar, two per bale, penetrating the full height of the wall. This technique provides no wall stiffening until the whole wall is up.
3. No pins. In a loadbearing building, once the roof load is on the bales, the pins may not be of much further value for resisting lateral forces. Additional testing is needed here.

Starting with the fourth course drive two, 5-ft [1.5 m] long pins per bale (#4 rebar, fiberglass rebar, sharpened bamboo rods or saplings, yucca stalks, wooden stakes, or salvaged conduit, pipe, or the equivalent)

rebar staples connecting corner bales

rebar "imbalers" in foundation

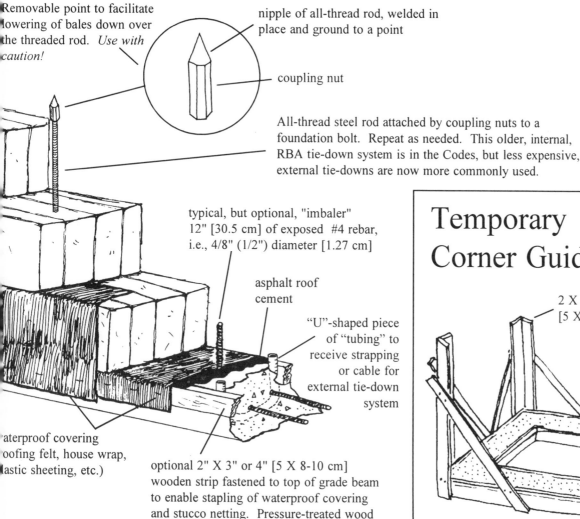

Removable point to facilitate lowering of bales down over the threaded rod. *Use with caution!*

nipple of all-thread rod, welded in place and ground to a point

coupling nut

All-thread steel rod attached by coupling nuts to a foundation bolt. Repeat as needed. This older, internal, RBA tie-down system is in the Codes, but less expensive, external tie-downs are now more commonly used.

typical, but optional, "imbaler" 12" [30.5 cm] of exposed #4 rebar, i.e., 4/8" (1/2") diameter [1.27 cm]

asphalt roof cement

"U"-shaped piece of "tubing" to receive strapping or cable for external tie-down system

waterproof covering (roofing felt, house wrap, plastic sheeting, etc.)

optional 2" X 3" or 4" [5 X 8-10 cm] wooden strip fastened to top of grade beam to enable stapling of waterproof covering and stucco netting. Pressure-treated wood preferred.

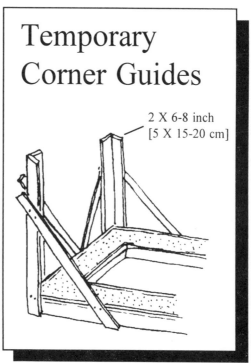

Temporary Corner Guides

2 X 6-8 inch [5 X 15-20 cm]

Rules of Thumb for Laying Bales

1. Start with good bales. <u>I</u>nspect each bale before placing it on the wall. Straighten if necessary. Use really "bad" bales for flakes.

2. **Know the details of the wall you are working on.** Consult, often, the wall map posted in front of your wall.

3. **Start laying at corners and door frames; later at window frames.** Leave a small gap between the frame and the adjacent bale. Regularly check frames for level.

4. **Monitor corners carefully to keep them vertical** (or sloping slightly inward). Secure corners with staples or by tying.

5. **Never cram a bale or a flake into place**; cramming can push corner bales out of position and can bend inward the sides of door and window frames, or push them out of square. **Take your time; pay attention to details.**

7. **When a whole course is finished, stomp the bales down into place.**
This gets some of the wall settling done immediately.

8. **Before starting each new course of bales, gently fill with loose straw all gaps or depressions** between bales, and any gaps between bales and frames.

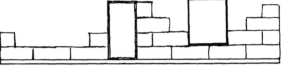

Angled Openings

Narrow openings let in less sunlight and restrict the view.

Angled openings let more sunlight in while enhancing the view.

Making Angled Bales

1. Create new shorter ties to allow for the bevel.
2. Add "keeper" strings that run to same new string on underside. These keep the new strings from sliding off the beveled end.
3. Cut original strings at knot and remove.
4. <u>Carefully</u> remove unwanted straw. A chainsaw, bow saw, or hay saw works well for this.

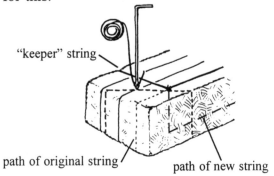

"keeper" string

path of original string

path of new string

Shortening a Bale Slightly

If you need to shorten a bale by only a small amount, try using this technique rather than installing three new strings. You can even shorten the exposed end of a bale that is already part of a wall (e.g., at a corner).

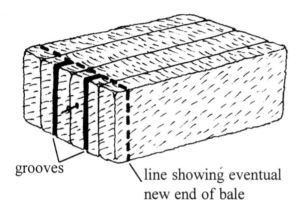

grooves

line showing eventual
new end of bale

1. Using a saw or grinder-mounted tool (see page 83), cut two grooves, as shown, to the required depth.
2. With the claw of a hammer, or the equivalent, remove the straw that is between the two grooves.
3. Using a large nail, or the equivalent, tighten the middle string, by twisting the nail, until it is as tight as the outside strings. Tie the nail to the string to prevent untwisting.
4. Repeat these steps with one outside string, then the other.

Kinky Bale-Laying Options

Super Shelf

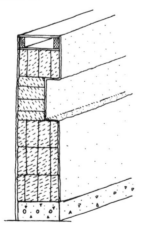

In a loadbearing wall, the on-edge bale should be centered on the bale below.

Instant Niche

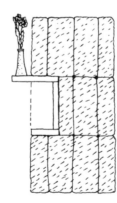

one bale high,
one bale long

Slab of straw cut off with a chainsaw before bale put in place.

Step 4. Roof-Bearing Assemblies

Challenge: First, to have previously selected, from a wide variety of options, the combination of roof-bearing assembly (RBA) and tie-down system that is "right" for you and for your design. Second, to get the segments of your RBA safely up onto the wall (unless you have chosen to create the RBA in place, on top of the wall) and to make strong connections where they meet. Third, to "tie" this assembly to the foundation in such a way that the maximum expected wind velocity (a.k.a. the design wind load) cannot turn the RBA/roof into an ILFO (identified low-flying object).

Walk-Through 🌲

• *During the process of finalizing your design and creating plans, you will have selected the type of RBA to be used. Among the factors that can influence this decision are:*

—whether the RBA will act as a lintel over openings; [This would allow you to use less wood in creating the nonbearing door and window frames, but may bring you to use more wood in the RBA itself. It will guarantee a straight, and probably level, roof line, but may limit the number and size of openings, since the load is concentrated on the bale columns between openings.]

—the distance between the points on the RBA at which the trusses/rafters/vigas/ wooden I-beams concentrate the roof load, the magnitude of the load at each point and whether it is the same for each point;

—the degree of compactness of the bales that the RBA will rest on;

—and, your various concerns about the materials required for the different options (e.g., regional availability for purchase or scavenging, cost [planetary and pecuniary], the tools and skills required to work with them).

You will have also decided whether it will extend continuously around the structure. Every wall carrying any roof load will need an RBA, but modern roof designs for square and rectangular buildings very seldom bear on more than two of the four walls (assuming a square or rectangular building). Even so, one might still choose to have the RBA be a continuous collar, in order to tie the whole building together. A rigid, continuous RBA could also serve as the lintel over all door and window openings in the building, thus enabling all the frames to be similar (lightweight, non-loadbearing). It would also distribute some of the roof load (otherwise carried entirely by the columns of bales between the openings in two of the walls) onto the other two walls.

There are, however, advantages to having the RBA discontinuous (i.e., only on the two loadbearing walls). It saves labor and the cost of materials (both to the planet and the wallet). If the roof design is a gable, and if bales are going to be used to fill in the eaves (the triangular areas formed by the sloping roof surfaces), builders often put in a light-weight horizontal stiffener at the level of the separate RBA's, before stacking bales to fill the triangles. If securely fastened at both ends to the RBA's, it can provide some of the collar-benefit of a continuous RBA. For more on stiffeners, see page 130.

• *Before you can fabricate your RBA, you must decide how to dimension it. It is typical to make the width slightly less than the average width of the bales. This ensures that the RBA, which generally acts as the nailer for the stucco netting, does not extend out beyond the edge of the bale wall at any point. Choosing the length dimensions is more complicated. There are two obvious approaches, each with potential advantages:*

1) Use the foundation dimensions, taking into consideration whatever setback you want to have from the edge of the bales. The advantages to this approach are that you can finish building all the segments of the RBA before the wall-raising is finished, that any pre-ordered trusses are guaranteed to fit , as planned, on it; and that you will be mightily motivated to end up with dimensions at the top of the wall that are real close to those at the bottom.

2) Use the actual dimensions of the top of your finished walls as your starting point. The advantage to this approach is that you can customize both the width and length dimensions to accommodate the actual shape and dimensions of your wall top (if this is your first building, you will be lucky not to end up with walls that flare out a little). Possible disadvantages are that you must leave some segments of the RBA unbuilt until the walls are finished, and that you may not be able (depending on their design) to pre-order trusses.

♣ *For the type of RBA on our "model" building, fabricate the roof bearing assembly on the ground in transportable sections. Then move these sections to the top of the wall and connect them, taking care to get strong connections between sections (especially at corners). Make sure that the diagonals are also as nearly equal as possible*

and that the walls are properly aligned and secured under the RBA. If your system for keeping the top of the wall centered under the RBA involves putting holes in whatever is acting as the waterproof cap, be sure to carefully seal any openings through which water could get down into the bales.

♣ *Unless your RBA already adequately protects the top of the walls from invasion by rodents, deny them access by utilizing various materials (e.g., cement-based mortar, metal lath, sheet metal, plywood scraps, old boards) alone or in combination.*

♣ *With your wall tops positioned, as appropriate, under the RBA and with the chosen mechanism in place to keep them in this position, "tie" the RBA securely to the foundation. For our "model", we have chosen an external tie-down system (e.g., polyester cord strapping with buckles or crimped seals). "U"-shaped pieces of "tubing" (e.g., irrigation distribution line, salvaged hose), positioned at a chosen interval in the foundation, provide sleeves for the strapping. You will, hopefully, have taken steps to ensure that no concrete could get into the tubing when you were doing your pour.*

Straight pieces of plastic pipe, passing horizontally through a "collar" type foundation, have also been used for sleeves. However, even with bevels created at the openings where the strapping cord emerges, the right-angle bend may put unwanted, extra stress on the strapping at these points.

Regardless of the type of sleeve used, however, care must also be taken to ensure that sharp corners have been eliminated where the strapping passes over the RBA. Small pieces of sheet metal, bent to make a right angle, work well. Or, you can buy pre-bent metal gizmos (e.g., Simpson A35s) at a construction supply yard.

Options for RBA's

Least Rigid

| Bamboo | Plank or TJI | Beam | Single 2"X6"* Ladder | 2 Sheets of Plywood or OSB |

More Rigid

* Could be used with loadbearing window frames and angle iron to stiffen it over a non-loadbearing door frame.

| Double 2"X6" Ladder | TJI and 2"X6" | Mongolian (see next page) |

| Two 2"X6"s w/2"X4" cleats | 2"X6", 2"X4" w/ continuous plywood "web" | 2"X6" w/ plywood |

Most Rigid

| TJI with plywood (closed box) | 2"X6" w/ plywood (closed box) | Concrete Bond Beam (added weight will shorten permissible spans; see page 31) |

Note: 2" X 4" [5 X 10 cm] and 2" X 6" [5 X 15 cm]

Some Examples of RBAs

Truss Joist I-Beam (TJI) Box

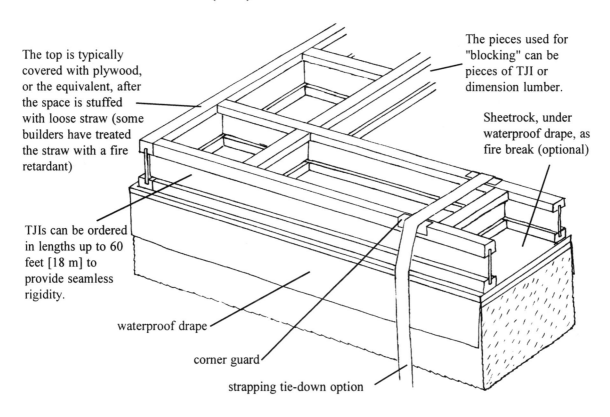

The top is typically covered with plywood, or the equivalent, after the space is stuffed with loose straw (some builders have treated the straw with a fire retardant)

The pieces used for "blocking" can be pieces of TJI or dimension lumber.

Sheetrock, under waterproof drape, as fire break (optional)

TJIs can be ordered in lengths up to 60 feet [18 m] to provide seamless rigidity.

waterproof drape

corner guard

strapping tie-down option

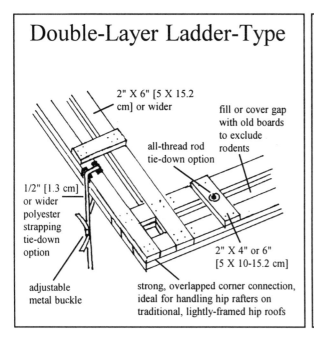

Double-Layer Ladder-Type

2" X 6" [5 X 15.2 cm] or wider

fill or cover gap with old boards to exclude rodents

all-thread rod tie-down option

1/2" [1.3 cm] or wider polyester strapping tie-down option

adjustable metal buckle

2" X 4" or 6" [5 X 10-15.2 cm]

strong, overlapped corner connection, ideal for handling hip rafters on traditional, lightly-framed hip roofs

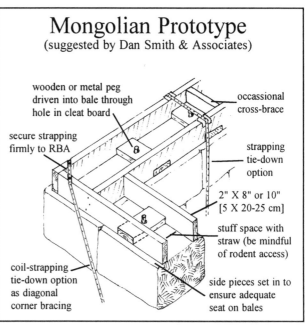

Mongolian Prototype
(suggested by Dan Smith & Associates)

wooden or metal peg driven into bale through hole in cleat board

occassional cross-brace

secure strapping firmly to RBA

strapping tie-down option

2" X 8" or 10" [5 X 20-25 cm]

stuff space with straw (be mindful of rodent access)

coil-strapping tie-down option as diagonal corner bracing

side pieces set in to ensure adequate seat on bales

Seismic Considerations

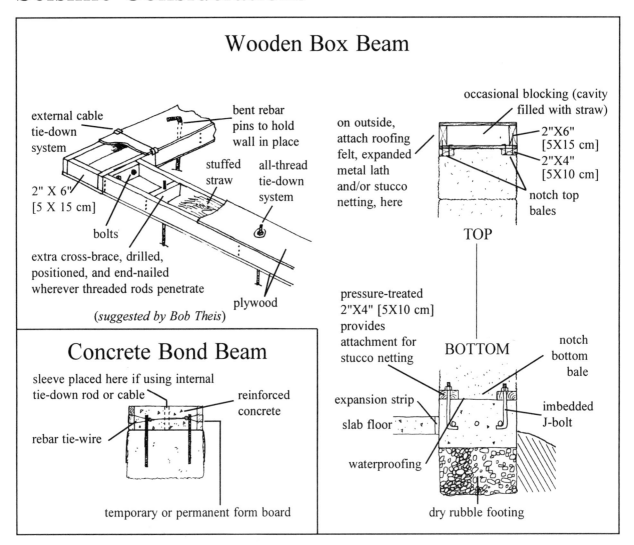

Wooden Box Beam

external cable tie-down system

bent rebar pins to hold wall in place

2" X 6" [5 X 15 cm]

stuffed straw

all-thread tie-down system

bolts

extra cross-brace, drilled, positioned, and end-nailed wherever threaded rods penetrate

plywood

(suggested by Bob Theis)

on outside, attach roofing felt, expanded metal lath and/or stucco netting, here

occasional blocking (cavity filled with straw)

2"X6" [5X15 cm]

2"X4" [5X10 cm]

notch top bales

TOP

pressure-treated 2"X4" [5X10 cm] provides attachment for stucco netting

BOTTOM

notch bottom bale

expansion strip

slab floor

imbedded J-bolt

waterproofing

dry rubble footing

Concrete Bond Beam

sleeve placed here if using internal tie-down rod or cable

reinforced concrete

rebar tie-wire

temporary or permanent form board

Filling the Gap Between Rigid RBA and Frames

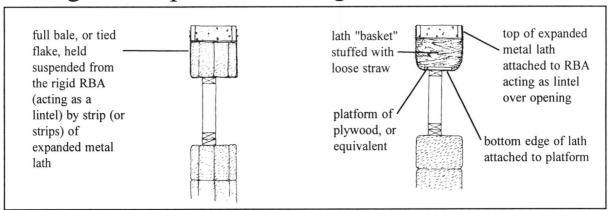

full bale, or tied flake, held suspended from the rigid RBA (acting as a lintel) by strip (or strips) of expanded metal lath

lath "basket" stuffed with loose straw

platform of plywood, or equivalent

top of expanded metal lath attached to RBA acting as lintel over opening

bottom edge of lath attached to platform

Tie-Down Systems:
General Considerations

In non-loadbearing designs, the framework that supports the roof load also ties the roof to the foundation, or to the ground, itself. Lacking this framework, loadbearing designs almost always include some mechanism to keep the roof from lifting off. In the historic Nebraska structures, metal or wooden stakes were driven at an angle down into the walls and the fastened to the rudimentary RBA. There is no evidence to indicate that this was not adequate for that situation (hipped roofs with minimal overhangs), but caution (and the concerns of engineers and building officials) have led most modern builders to create ties from the RBA to the foundation.

In a design involving no use of stucco netting, inside or out, the tie-down system (arguably) continues to perform an important function, even after the surface coating is in place. This will be especially true if seismic forces or differential settling of the foundation ever cracked this coating. If, however, cement-based plaster has been applied over stucco netting (especially if applied in vertical strips fastened securely to both the RBA and the foundation), any previously installed tie-down system is then relegated to a strictly backup role. This assumes, of course, that the structural integrity of this plaster-membrane tie-down remains intact for the life-span of the building. For description of a system that uses stucco netting as the only tie-down (Look, Ma, no backup!), see page 73.

Several builders have experimented with placing the tie-down system outside the stucco netting, to hold the curtain of netting against the bales. Through-ties, connecting the inner part to the outer part of a loop of wire, cable or strapping, would further increase the effectiveness of these loops, perhaps making any other tie-throughs unnecessary. One possible chronology for this idea would be as follows:

1) Attach vertically oriented strips of stucco netting to the RBA as soon as it is in place.

2) Insert lengths of strapping through sleeves in the foundation, passing one end of each length up over the RBA.

3) Fasten the two ends of each length together with a metal buckle, hand-tightening periodically to take the slack out of the strapping as the walls settle under the roof load.

4) When the settling is complete, and just before hand-tightening the strapping for the last time, pull down on the stucco netting and fasten it securely to a wooden nailer attached to the side or top of the foundation.

5) Now, hand tighten the strapping one last time.

6) Complete the process by creating some through-ties, to connect the strapping on the inside to that on the outside.

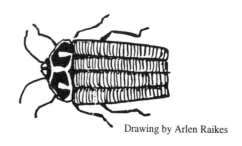

Drawing by Arlen Raikes

Tie-Down Options

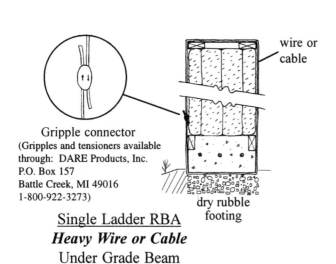

Gripple connector
(Gripples and tensioners available through: DARE Products, Inc.
P.O. Box 157
Battle Creek, MI 49016
1-800-922-3273)

wire or cable

dry rubble footing

Single Ladder RBA
Heavy Wire or Cable
Under Grade Beam

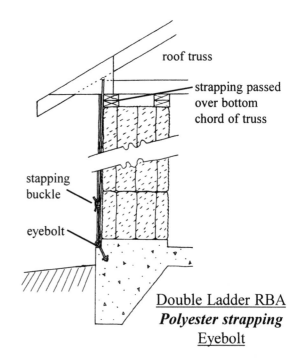

roof truss

strapping passed over bottom chord of truss

stapping buckle

eyebolt

Double Ladder RBA
Polyester strapping
Eyebolt

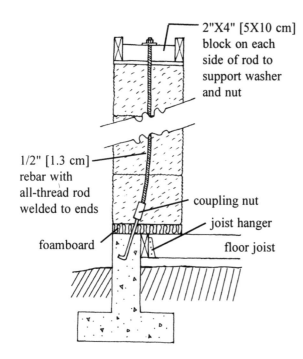

2"X4" [5X10 cm] block on each side of rod to support washer and nut

1/2" [1.3 cm] rebar with all-thread rod welded to ends

coupling nut

joist hanger

foamboard

floor joist

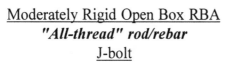

Moderately Rigid Open Box RBA
"All-thread" rod/rebar
J-bolt

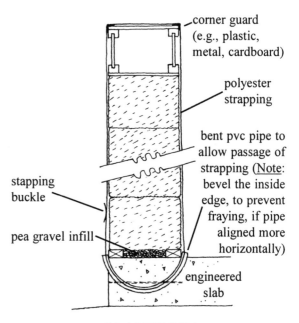

corner guard (e.g., plastic, metal, cardboard)

polyester strapping

bent pvc pipe to allow passage of strapping (Note: bevel the inside edge, to prevent fraying, if pipe aligned more horizontally)

stapping buckle

pea gravel infill

engineered slab

Rigid TJI RBA
Polyester strapping
PVC pipe in grade beam

Tie-Down Strength and Spacing - Assessing What is Needed

It's easy to guesstimate that a shed roof with no overhangs, on a small building, might need no other tie-down than its own weight. However, given a high profile roof, with large overhangs, on a large building, in an area with a design wind load of 120 mph (3.2 km/second), even the bravest (or most foolhardy) of us all might be reluctant to stake the stability of our roof on a guess.

To start with, we would want to know the maximum uplift that our tie-down system would conceivably have to resist. For a small, simple building, you may choose to do the calculation yourself, using formulas such as those provided in Cole and Wing (1976). Or, regardless of the size of the structure, you can have an engineer or architect do this for you. Once you know the number of pounds of upward force to be resisted by all the tie-downs along a given wall, divide this number by a conservative value for the safe working load for a given type of tie-down, to determine how many such tie-downs should be placed along that wall. Consider arranging the tie-downs in groups of two or three per location along the wall, thus reducing the number of sleeves or pieces of attachment hardware. Remember that one long piece of strapping, passed three times through a sleeve and over the RBA and then fastened, has far less strength than three separate loops fastened individually.

Manufacturers often provide information on the breaking strength (a.k.a. tensile strength) of things like cable and strapping, but seldom say whether it, or the connection (e.g., clamp, seal or buckle), will fail first. Talk to the technical representative at the company, and try to get her/him to provide the safe working load for the product as combined with the connector you wish to use.

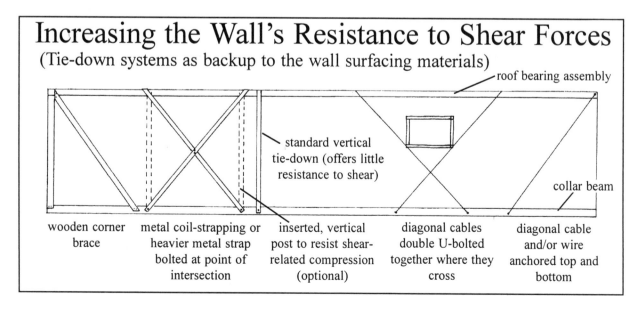

Increasing the Wall's Resistance to Shear Forces
(Tie-down systems as backup to the wall surfacing materials)

roof bearing assembly

standard vertical tie-down (offers little resistance to shear)

collar beam

| wooden corner brace | metal coil-strapping or heavier metal strap bolted at point of intersection | inserted, vertical post to resist shear-related compression (optional) | diagonal cables double U-bolted together where they cross | diagonal cable and/or wire anchored top and bottom |

Tie-Downs as Pre-Stressing Mechanisms

Modern builders, being the impatient souls that we are, have long dreamed of finding a simple way of using the tie-down system to pre-stress (i.e., mechanically compress) the walls, prior to putting the roof on. This would permit immediate application of exterior plaster to protect the walls. Ideally, the compressing mechanism would apply a load in excess of any eventual, combined dead and live loads, further stiffening the walls. Even with mud plaster (and perhaps without pinning) the walls could then withstand heavy wind loads without unacceptable deformation or cracking.

Starting with what was already being used for tie-downs, initial attempts were made to use the in-the-wall, threaded rod system to pull down the RBA, thereby pre-stressing the bales. Unfortunately, it was found that the threads would strip before sufficient compression had been achieved. Then, thanks to the sharp eye of Greenfire Institute's Ted Butchart, along came the Gripple. This small metal disc contains cams that allow a wire or cable to pass through the disc in one direction only. Combined with a tensioning tool, this offered the potential of using a loop of wire or cable to pull down on the RBA with enough force to pre-stress the walls. Unfortunately, at least when used with a rigid RBA, no individual loop can be tensioned enough to pull the whole RBA down significantly.

Hope was fading fast when, in the great tradition of the Royal Canadian Mounted Police, the barking of sled dogs was heard in the distance. Onto the scene, from Ottawa, came engineer Bob Platts and architect Linda Chapman, with an ingenious system that involves inflation.

Here's how it works. After building the walls without pins (but utilizing a system for temporary external bracing), they create a light, wood-frugal RBA, onto which they lay a long, narrow, inflatable tube. On this tube they lay a ladder-like assembly that has the equivalent of hooks sticking out on both sides. Having secured the bottom end of strips of wire netting to the foundation or toe-up, they then push the top end of each strip over the hooks. This is done both inside and out. Now the fun begins, as they slowly inflate the tube. Since the "ladder" can't go up (being held down by the netting), the RBA has to go down, compressing the bales as it does so. This arrangement has the tremendous advantage of applying the downward force both uniformly and simultaneously along the whole length of the RBA. Using numbers derived from the roof design, the live load for the location and structural testing, a target for compression is determined. When this amount of compression has been achieved, the netting is securely fastened to the sides of the RBA before the ladder and tube are removed.

Testing of pin-less walls, pre-stressed with this system, has shown them to be as resistant to wind loading (at right angles to the wall), as similarly pre-stressed walls pinned in the normal fashion (see *The Last Straw*, Issue No. 14, page 14). This suggests that, unless the pins in a pre-stressed wall contribute to the wall's shear strength (i.e., its resistance to being changed from a rectangle to a parallelogram), the pins are serving no structural purpose. Imagine not having to pin! For more information on this intriguing system, contact Bob and Linda at Fibrehouse Limited, 27 Third Ave., Ottawa, Ontario, Canada, K1S 2J5; tel/fax (613) 231-4690; e-mail: <fibre@freenet.carleton.ca>.

Step 5. Adding the Roof

Challenge: to create a sheltering cap (some combination of ceiling, and/or roof, and insulation) that 1) is securely attached to the roof-bearing assembly, 2) protects the tops of your walls and your interior spaces from the elements, 3) adequately retards the movement of heat, and 4) does this efficiently (re: cost, materials, labor).

Walk-Through

• *You will, of course, have chosen a particular roof shape during the design process. Our experience leads us to strongly favor shapes that will allow for overhangs (the wetter the climate, the bigger the overhang) and for guttering, to prevent splash back onto the base of the walls. Should dedication to a regional architectural style, personal preference, or deed restrictions "demand" the use of parapet walls (low extensions of the walls above the roof line), we suggest using a low-pitch, shed roof with parapets on only three sides (as illustrated on the next page). This enables water to move unimpeded off the roof, preferably into a gutter. Even then, very savvy detailing is needed to prevent any water from getting into the base of the parapet, and from there, down into the bales. For one architect's version of a (hopefully) leak proof parapet detail, see Issue 8, page 28, of* The Last Straw. *Although bales have sometimes been used to form the parapets, it is more common to frame them, using more wood but less waterproof membrane and plaster.*

♣ *Fabricate the central part of the roof skeleton, using identical homemade or commercial trusses. Complete the end hips, using hip trusses or traditional framing. Double up the two end trusses if your hip system concentrates extra load on them.*

♣ *Brace the roof skeleton as it grows, leaving this bracing permanently in place where appropriate.*

♣ *Securely attach all trusses (and any rafters) to the outside edge of the RBA using the appropriate connectors (a.k.a. hurricane ties or the equivalent). A strong tie-down system for the RBA will mean nothing if these attachments are weak.*

♣ *Attach 2" X 4" [5 X 10 cm] purlin strips, at 2' [0.6 m] intervals, to the roof framework.*

• *Fasten 26-gauge metal roofing to the purlins with special, self-tapping screws equipped with neoprene washers, using standard caulking strips where adjacent panels overlap.*

♣ *Create screened, louvered, attic vents in the gablets at each end of the roof peak, installing proper flashing where the bottom edge of the triangular gablet meets the sloping metal roof.*

If designs with gabled roofs, consider installing a prefabricated ridge vent to provide venting along the entire ridge line. ***Don't underestimate the value of adequate venting****. In hot climates (see Cook 1989), it will keep your house cooler. In cold climates (see Nisson and Dutt 1985; Lenchek et al. 1987), it will prevent problematical moisture buildup.*

♣ *Attach some material to the underside of the overhang created by the ends of the trusses/rafters, leaving adequate, screened vents to allow air movement up into the attic space.*

• *With the roof skin now in place, move inside and install any radiant heat barriers following manufacturer's directions. These barriers can be particularly effective in reducing cooling requirements in very hot climates. For an excellent overview of this option, see Nisson (1990).*

♣ *Install all necessary ducting, stove pipe brackets, electrical boxes (e.g., for overhead lights, smoke detectors, fans), wiring and plumbing in the attic space.*

♣ *Install the ceiling material(s) and insulate (or vice versa). Be sure to provide a way to easily gain access to the attic space. If the access is from a space that is heated or cooled, make sure that the removable panel is well-insulated.*

RED

Don't assume that just because your bale walls have a high R- or RSI-value, you can skimp on ceiling/roof insulation and have an energy-efficient building. *The bigger the building, the bigger the ceiling area relative to the total interior surface area of bale walls. For a building with 1200 square feet [111.5 square meters] of usable interior space and eight foot [2.44 m] high walls, the ceiling area is virtually the same as the wall area. For a larger building, the ceiling area will exceed that of the walls. It may not be cost-efficient to create as high an R-value [RSI-value] in the ceiling as you'll have in the walls, but do try to achieve the levels recommended for superinsulated designs for your climatic conditions. For recommendations, consult local architects/ designers that specialize in energy-efficient design, your state Energy Office or selected books (e.g., Nisson and Dutt 1985, Lenchek et al. 1987, Cook 1989, Lstiburek 1997).*

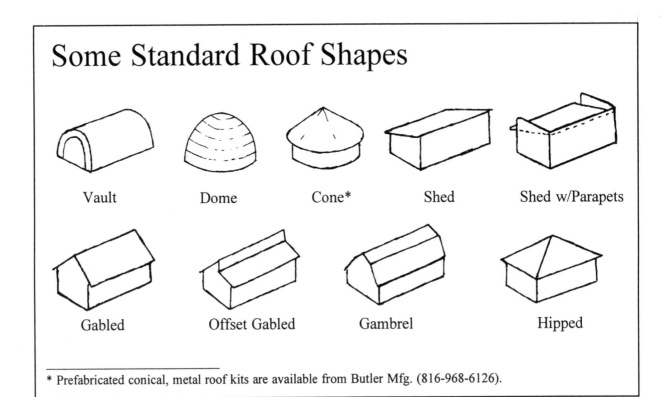

Some Standard Roof Shapes

Vault   Dome   Cone*   Shed   Shed w/Parapets

Gabled   Offset Gabled   Gambrel   Hipped

* Prefabricated conical, metal roof kits are available from Butler Mfg. (816-968-6126).

Dutch Hip Framing Options

This option is often used on rectangular buildings as a more interesting substitute for a gabled roof.

Depending on the framing system (three possibilities shown here), some roof weight can be distributed to the shorter end walls. This roof shape also overhangs all four walls. For detailed information on roof framing, see Gross (1984).

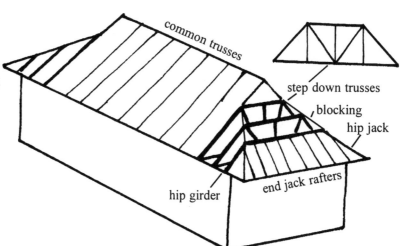

common trusses

step down trusses

blocking

hip jack

hip girder

end jack rafters

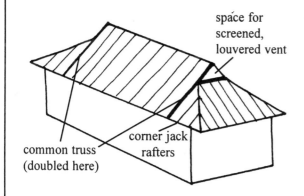

space for screened, louvered vent

common truss (doubled here)

corner jack rafters

Historically, square or nearly-square bale-walled buildings were covered with a lightly-framed hip roof. The advantage is the nearly equal distribution of roof weight on all four walls.

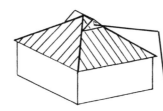

A short ridge can be scabbed on to modify the pyramidal profile and provide for adequate venting of the attic space (a very important consideration).

Two-Story, Loadbearing Options Using Super-Trusses™

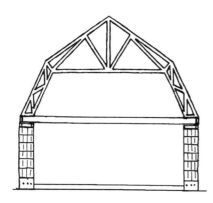

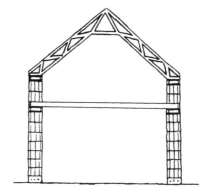

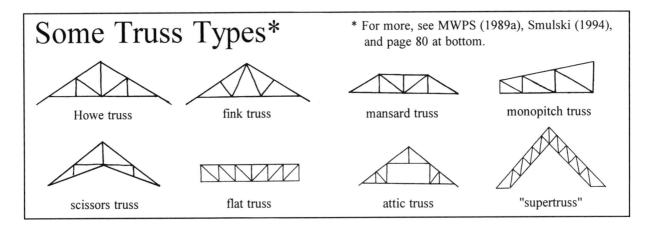

Some Truss Types*

* For more, see MWPS (1989a), Smulski (1994), and page 80 at bottom.

Howe truss   fink truss   mansard truss   monopitch truss

scissors truss   flat truss   attic truss   "supertruss"

Roof Surface Options

A secure and durable roof surface is vital for the long-term structural health of your straw-bale home. Periodic maintenance and eventual replacement are also very important. Many historic Nebraska structures died from "roof failure". For roof surfacing options, see Herbert (1989), Kolle (1995), and Malin (1995c).

Among the many roofing surfaces that have been used on bale buildings are:

• Metal (pricey, but easy to install and durable). This typically means standard galvanized or color-coated panels. In dry climates, the shallow-corrugated, cold-rolled steel decking, normally used in high-rise construction as form work for poured concrete floors, provides an interesting alternative. It comes ungalvanized (i.e., without a zinc coating) and quickly attains an attractive, rusted surface. We would not, however, recommend its use in wetter climates, especially those characterized by acid rain. For more information on this option, call The Myers Group at 1-800-729-3325.

• Single-ply membranes (pricey, tricky to install, but effective even on roofs with very little slope, if correctly installed) (see Loomis 1991).

• Asphalt-impregnated roll roofing (inexpensive, easy to install, visually boring).

• Asphalt-impregnated, fake-shingle strips (more work than roll roofing, but less boring).

• Shakes (either wood or composite materials).

• Tile (pricey and **heavy**). Due to their weight, tiles are not normally used in loadbearing designs. Traditionally, "tile" meant fired clay, but tiles made from tires, concrete, and composite materials are now available. The latter can contain considerable amounts of recycled materials.

• Living roofs (ARCHIBIO 1995b, 1995c).

• Thatch (e.g., palm leaves, grass).

• Tarps (especially suited to vaults). Although requiring periodic replacement, tarps can provide a cost-effective, though none too pretty, option.

Some of the less obvious factors that might influence your choice of roof surfaces may include the following:

• The potability of water harvested off different surfaces. Most types of tile and commercial steel roofing panels are favored over products containing asphalt.

• The weight of the material per unit area. Given some maximum load per square foot of loadbearing wall-top, lighter materials will permit longer spans.

• Degree of flammability. Not generally considered an important factor, but of vital importance in certain areas where the likelihood of brush or forest fires is great.

• The stylistic appropriateness for the neighborhood and/or region.

A Simple Straw-Bale Roof Idea

A long-held desire of many straw-bale aficionados has been to reduce the amount of wood used, while retaining adequate insulation. Vaults and domes can work. Another idea, using ferro-cement and an elastomeric coating, is shown at right.

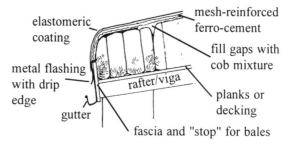

elastomeric coating

mesh-reinforced ferro-cement

fill gaps with cob mixture

metal flashing with drip edge

rafter/viga

planks or decking

gutter

fascia and "stop" for bales

The Shed Roof Option

Due perhaps to its lack of visual pizzazz, the simple, low-pitch, shed roof is generally shunned by both architects and owner-designer-builders. With a few porches, however, this ugly duckling takes on a modest charm. And for the owner-builder, at least in regions where snow loads are minimal, it offers some attractive advantages:

• If we exclude the flat roof (dumb, dumb, dumb) and the very low, gabled roof (why bother?, and few do), it covers a given structure with the minimum square footage of roof surface. Less materials, less labor, less cost.

• With a single gutter and down spout, all the water harvested off the roof can be channeled safely away from the base of the walls onto vegetation, or into a cistern for storage.

• As with a gabled roof constructed with triangular trusses, the whole roof structure is made up of a single, repeated element. Once you've got the first one attached correctly, all the rest are "no-brainers".

• If 14 inches [35.6 cm], or more, high "truss joist I's" (a.k.a. TJI's, wooden I-beams) are used, long spans are possible, with adequate space available for

superinsulation. They can be ordered in various heights and in custom lengths far greater than you'll ever need.

Wooden I-Beam (TJI)

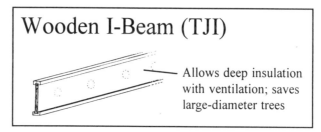

Allows deep insulation with ventilation; saves large-diameter trees

• The necessity of having one end of the TJI's, or rafters, higher than the other, provides the opportunity to insert clerestory windows directly under the roof, where they can be easily shaded by a modest overhang.

Shed Roof Rafter Details

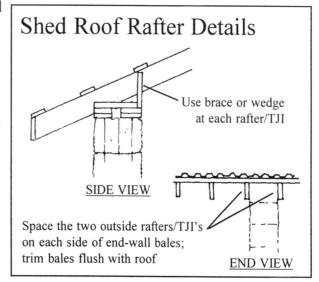

Use brace or wedge at each rafter/TJI

SIDE VIEW

Space the two outside rafters/TJI's on each side of end-wall bales; trim bales flush with roof

END VIEW

Options for Ceiling Materials

• <u>Sheet rock</u> (a.k.a. drywall, gyp board). This old standard is cheap, relatively non-toxic, and fire-resistant. It is also heavy and cumbersome to install overhead without specialized equipment. For tips on how-to, see Ferguson (1996). To get a continuous, smooth surface, ready for painting, one must fill the joints and sand the filler material smooth. No one we've ever met seems to enjoy the last-mentioned step, and many flat-out hate it. Some builders avoid this step by filling the joints, staining the ceiling with a cheap, dark stain and then stapling rolls of reed or split-bamboo fencing to the ceiling. The long, black-coated staples used for telephone wire installation work well, and are nearly invisible, but do require a special staple gun.

• <u>Wood</u> in various forms. Depending on your design, your wood may be attached to the bottom of something (e.g., a none-too-pretty, pre-engineered truss) or on top of something that you want to see (e.g., a handsome round or squarish beam). People have used:
  —Commercial tongue and groove planking
  —Stained or singed plywood, or the equivalent. An unusual option here is WheatSheet, a hard, paneling material made by binding wheat straw with a resin. For info, contact Naturall (*sic*) Fiber Board, Box 175, Minneapolis, KS 67467; 913-392-9922.
  —Rough cut planks. Something like black plastic sheeting, placed on the upper surface of the planks, will both provide an air/vapor barrier and keep fragments of your insulation from dribbling down through the inevitable cracks into your caviar.
  —Peeled saplings (a.k.a. *lattias*), cane, bamboo, etc. Rather than placing them at right angles to the beams , one can angle them and reverse the direction between each consecutive beam to form an attractive "herringbone" pattern.

• <u>PGB3</u>. This unusual product, consisting almost entirely of compressed straw, comes in sheets that are four feet by eight feet by one and a half inches. The surface has a lot of texture and gives the board the properties of an acoustical panel (for info contact BioFab at (916)243-4032 or e-mail them at <info@strawboard.com>).

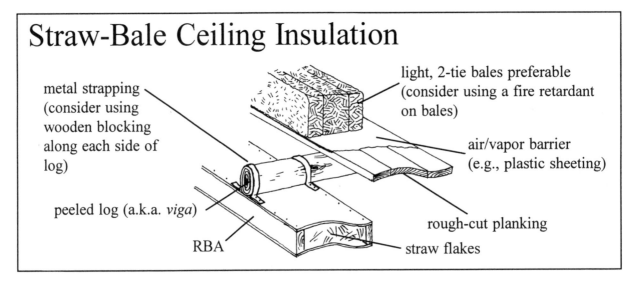

Straw-Bale Ceiling Insulation

metal strapping (consider using wooden blocking along each side of log)

peeled log (a.k.a. *viga*)

RBA

light, 2-tie bales preferable (consider using a fire retardant on bales)

air/vapor barrier (e.g., plastic sheeting)

rough-cut planking

straw flakes

Ceiling Insulation Options

For unbiased articles comparing common types of insulation, see Wilson (1995a; 1996). A wide variety of options have been used, including:

• Fiberglass, in several forms.

• Cellulose, from recycled newspaper, in several forms.

• Cotton fibers, from recycled fabric trimmings, in several forms.

• Foam board

• Structural, insulative panels (for a combined ceiling and roof). Typically these panels have foam sandwiched between two sheets of oriented strand-board (a.k.a., OSB). An interesting alternative, made with straw between the sheets, is being manufacture by Agriboard. Call them at (515) 472-0363 or e-mail them at <agriboard@lisco.com>.

• Loose straw, flakes or bales, including bales used both as the structural roof and the insulation in domes and vaults (see Lerner 1997). Especially when using loose straw, it is advisable to first treat the straw with a fire retardant. For specific information on retardants, see page 19. One approach to treating loose straw has been to first immerse it in the solution and then spread it out on tarps or a concrete slab for drying. If your retardant is water soluble, you must re-treat the straw if it is rained before you get it under roof.

• Surplus sleeping bags containing "fiberfill". Sometimes bought very cheaply (from the U.S. Forest Service), and stacked several high, they are performing well in one small structure in New Mexico. Human ingenuity at its best, we'd say.

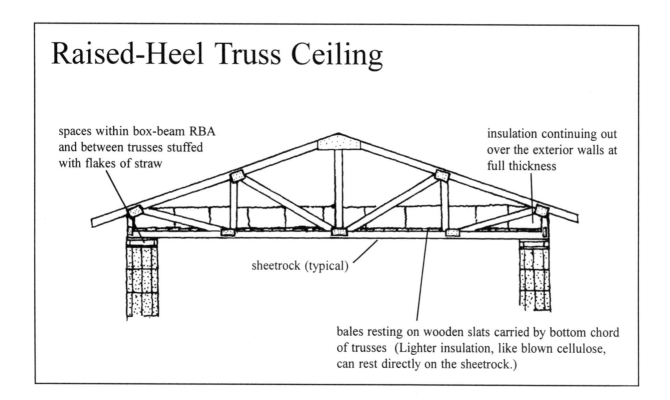

Raised-Heel Truss Ceiling

spaces within box-beam RBA and between trusses stuffed with flakes of straw

insulation continuing out over the exterior walls at full thickness

sheetrock (typical)

bales resting on wooden slats carried by bottom chord of trusses (Lighter insulation, like blown cellulose, can rest directly on the sheetrock.)

Step 6. Letting the Walls Compress

Challenge: to patiently allow the bale walls to complete their compressional response to the "dead load" exerted by the RBA/roof/ceiling/insulation system, and to use this opportunity to work comfortably inside your building on a variety of tasks.

Walk-Through 🌳

♣ *Unless your design includes a tie-down system that enables mechanical compression (see page 73), you must now let the walls gradually compress. Select two, or more, points along each wall at which to periodically measure the distance from the top of the toe-up (or floor surface) to the top of the RBA (or, later, the bottom of the ceiling surface). Number the locations and record the measured distances such that you can compare each set of measurements to the previous set. For two different approaches to measurement, each reflecting for a different degree of anal retentivity, see page 86.*

The initial response to loading is rapid, but then begins to taper off. Experience suggests that complete compression may require anywhere from three to about six weeks. Depending on initial bale compaction and roof weight, total compression will vary from some fraction of an inch (a cm or less) to several inches (about five or six cm). During the settling period, you should occasionally adjust your tie-downs to remove any slack. When all of the measurements in a set show no change from the previous set, you can safely proceed with surfacing the walls, as described in Step 7.

♣ *With the tops of the bale walls now protected by the new roof and the bottom course sitting safely up off the ground on a toed-up, waterproofed foundation and draped*

with a waterproof membrane, you can catch your breath. Use this respite for things like:

—recreating and reconnecting with loved ones;

—tweaking any ornery bales into final position;

—adjusting the verticality of door and window frames, as needed, and connecting them securely to the bale walls with dowels or metal pins;

—installing the doors and windows;

—and, creating the floor, if this has not already been done. If the bales have been stacked on a wooden deck carried by basement walls, stem walls or piers/columns, the floor is already in place. Similarly, a slab-on-grade creates the floor and the foundation with a single "pour" of concrete.

Although the floor may end up being created at different points in different buildings, we have chosen to deal with the question of insulation under floors in just two places – right here and on page 88, where we illustrate several options. During the design process, you should have made a decision whether or not to insulate and if so, with what and to what degree. Among the things that you might consider are listed below:

1. The regional climate and the micro-climate at your site.

2. The type, or types, of floor you have chosen.

3. Whether the floor will be heated and/or cooled by pipes through which water or, less

commonly, air will be circulated.

4. Whether you are using a frost-protected, shallow foundation, since floor insulation can increase the amount of insulation required at the perimeter (see HUD 1995).

5. The calculated or guesstimated payback time for the investment, and the planetary costs of not doing it.

Our "model" building has a high-mass floor created within the above-grade collar. We are using no insulation around the perimeter of our foundation or under our floor, since our "model" climate requires very little heating or cooling.

The finished floor surface should be at least 1.5" [3.9 cm] below the top of the collar to protect the bales from any interior flooding. We have specified a high-mass floor so that winter sunlight (i.e., solar radiation), entering through south-facing glazing, can hit, and be absorbed by, the floor. This daytime storage of heat will prevent room air temperatures from becoming uncomfortably high during the day. At night, this same heat will "bleed" back out, helping to keep the space from becoming undesirably cool.

—Creating non-loadbearing interior partitions, leaving an adequate gap above them to allow for the settling that may still take place. An alternative approach is to postpone creation of the interior partitions, with any incorporated plumbing and wiring, until the interior surfacing is in place on the exterior bale walls. Then, with all the surfacing materials in place (and all the compressing finished), you no longer needs to guess how much of a gap to leave to allow for settling.

This approach also minimizes the amount of patching required if one eventually relocates a partition wall. See pages 85-87

for options regarding the creation and attachment of partition walls.

—Extending the plumbing into, or up into the interior space. If you do choose to install some, or all, of the partitions at this point, you can also complete any plumbing that belongs in them (see Massey 1994).

There are two obvious ways to get any water lines (cold or hot) into your straw-bale house. The first is to bring any pipes in under your foundation/footings and leave them "stubbed out" at the appropriate locations when you create the floor. If a problem ever develops with one of these buried pipes, you will either destroy part of your floor (if you can pinpoint the leak) or, more likely, abandon all piping under the floor The logical thing to do then, is to consider using the second option, which you might have been better off using to begin with.

*That involves bringing the pipe that provides cold water to the structure up out of the ground outside the wall, at one or more locations opposite a single fixture (e.g., a kitchen sink), or opposite an interior "plumbing wall", preferably framed with 2"X6" [5X15 cm] lumber. Skillful, careful use of the tip of a small chain saw will create a hole, sloped slightly upward toward the inside, for a "sleeve" of plastic pipe. Insert the sleeve and plug any space around it with your cob mixture. The pipe(s) can then be plumbed through the bale wall and into the frame wall. **To safely use this option, you must be able to insulate the pipes to prevent freezing, even during record low temperatures.** In colder climates this may not be economically possible.*

If you cannot avoid running water pipes along straw-bale walls, at least isolate them

carefully and completely from the straw.
—Equipping the straw-bale walls with
wooden elements to enable the hanging of
cabinets, bookcases, etc. If these elements
will be hidden by the plaster, map their
position precisely on a diagram and save it
for later use. We'll cover some of the various
options for hanging things on straw-bale
walls in Step 8.

   —Installing, in any partitions created at
this point and in the exterior walls, any phone
jacks, antenna cable, electrical boxes and
wiring (see Traister 1994, Cauldwell 1996).

   —Rounding/trimming off bales at exterior
corners and at door and window openings, as
desired, to provide for a "soft-profile"
finished appearance. This is also the time to
trim off any undesired protrusions on your
wall surfaces (a line trimmer/"weed whacker"
works beautifully for this). Any niches,
notches, alcoves, etc., should all be created at
this time using a small chain saw or, better
yet, a small electric grinder, equipped with a
cable-twist, flat wire wheel or a cutting wheel
with chainsaw teeth on the circumference
(called the Lancelot). Both are illustrated
below. The wire wheels are cheaper and

never require sharpening, but (arguably) cut
a little less quickly. They are available from
welding supply stores. If none of your local
hardware stores, or specialty tool suppliers,
carry the Lancelot, contact King Arthur Tools
at (800) 942-1300.

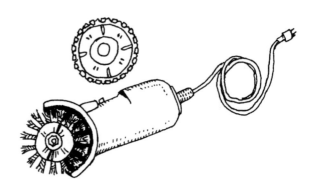

**When using any of the above mentioned
tools to cut straw, you should always wear
safety goggles and a dust mask** (does
someone have to die from "yellow-lung
disease" before this becomes automatic?).
Chainsaws, grinders and even line trimmers
are dangerous tools, capable of doing major
damage to the operator or those nearby. Use
them only with great care.

Niches and Counter-Niches

(idea from Bill & Kalla Buchholz)

(idea from Jon Ruez)

Bale Tweaking Tools

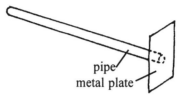

pipe
metal plate

6" X 6" X 10"
[1.5 X 1.5 X 25.4 cm]

<u>Big Sledge</u>

<u>Wooden Maul</u>
handle mounted in hole or on side

<u>Tamper/"Persuader"</u>

Wiring Options

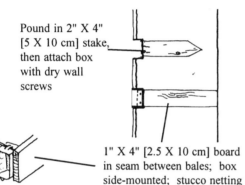

Pound in 2" X 4"
[5 X 10 cm] stake,
then attach box
with dry wall
screws

1" X 4" [2.5 X 10 cm] board
in seam between bales; box
side-mounted; stucco netting
can be attached to both ends.

- Wires in metal or flexible plastic conduit on wall surface; or in groove (dug with claw hammer, or cut with tip of chainsaw or circular saw); or run under floor and "popped up" to boxes.
- Wires in surfaced-mounted "decorator" conduit (attached after the wall has been surfaced).
- Plastic-sheathed cable (e.g., Romex 12/2) pushed into 2 1/4" [5.7 cm]-deep groove cut into walls. Hold in place with "Roberta pins" (see page 92).
- Cable run horizontally on a bale course during wall raising. Position wires about 3" [7.6 cm] from the inner edge of the bales to prevent risk of hitting them when pinning).

If doing your own electrical, see Traister (1994) and Cauldwell (1996); Re: EMFs from wiring, see Pinsky (1995).

RED

High-Mass Floor Options

- Bricks or blocks (e.g., fired adobes) on sand (see Ring 1990), stone on earth (Laporte 1993)
- Tiles on slab
- Earth (see Laporte 1993, Steen et al. 1994, Steen and Steen 1997b, and several articles in Issue 17 of *The Last Straw*)
- Compacted soil-cement / rammed earth (see Berglund 1985, McHenry 1989, Easton 1996)
- Concrete
  —regular slab-on-grade
  —regular slab poured over bale insulation (see illustration on page 88)
  —scored or embossed slab (pressed-in pattern)
  —large, thick, poured-in-place "tiles" (frame stays in place)

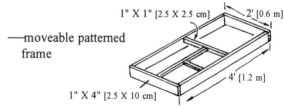

—moveable patterned frame

1" X 1" [2.5 X 2.5 cm]   2' [0.6 m]

4' [1.2 m]

1" X 4" [2.5 X 10 cm]

Coloring Concrete

- Mix dye with the concrete before pouring.
- Sprinkle on and "float" in during final finishing.
- Staining: commercial or homemade (artist pigments, or use ferrous sulphate which is cheap and available from agricultural, chemical, or fertilizer suppliers to get a yellowish, reddish brown).
- Apply special concrete paints.

Options for Interior Partitions

• **Standard frame** (2"X 4" [5X10 cm] or 2"X6" [5X15.2 cm]), covered with sheetrock or some other type of paneling. You may want to use WheatSheet, a thin panel made entirely from straw and a formaldehyde-free, polymer-based binder. For access information, see "Options for Ceiling Materials" on page 79.

• **Infilled standard or widely spaced frame** to which stucco netting has been attached on both sides, creating cavities that are stuffed with straw. Paster is then applied to the resulting surface with hand or trowel, producing an undulating surface reminiscent of the finished bale walls.

Another infill option would involve tamping "light clay/straw" mix into the space between formboards temporarily attached to the frame (see Laporte 1993).

• **Shipping pallets** that have been stuffed with flakes of straw (for sound insulation) before being stacked and connected to form a partition wall. A thick coat of earth plaster, well keyed into the spaces between the boards, will probably stay on just fine without stucco netting. Pallets which would otherwise take up scarce space in a landfill, can usually be acquired without money changing hands. The planet will love you for converting a waste material into a free resource.

• **Wattle and daub**. The "wattle" is a woven framework of saplings, bamboo, reeds, etc., intertwined with smaller twigs or branches. The daub is usually earth plaster, smeared onto both sides of the panel.

• **Hanging dividers**. If the only function of a specific divider is to provide visual privacy, why spend a lot of time and money building a heavy, "permanent" partition that you'll probably end up wanting to move eventually.

Consider hanging a fabric partition from those little gizmos that slide along a metal track attached to the ceiling. This system saves space, while providing visual privacy when needed.

• **Furniture walls**. As above, floor standing elements like bookcases and storage units can be used to provide visual privacy without creating a permanent monument to over-building.

• **Earth materials**.

—*Adobe* (McHenry 1989, Houlen and Guillard 1994) and *Cob* (Bee 1997, Smith 1997) can be used to create handsome, relatively narrow (8" [20.3 cm] is a suggested minimum), sound- dampening walls that also contribute to the thermal mass within the bale envelope. No matter where situated, they will contribute to the effectiveness of passive and active cooling strategies, but are of less benefit in passive solar heating strategies unless they receive <u>direct</u> sunlight for a significant part of the winter day. For specific suggestions on combining earth materials with straw bales in your design, see Issue 17 of *The Last Straw*.

—*Rammed earth* (Easton 1996) is seldom considered for a partition wall unless the wall will also be carrying roof weight, as in the hybrid design with the inverted trusses on page 22, bottom left.

• **Straw bales**. Whole bales, either flat or on edge, have seldom been used for interior partitions, since the resulting walls (ditto for rammed earth) take up lots of precious space. Three-tie bales converted into four-tie bales that are then cut in half, would reduce the straw thickness to about 11" [28 cm]. A wall made from these "straw slabs", perhaps sandwiched between 2"X6" [5X15.2 cm]

Matts' Method

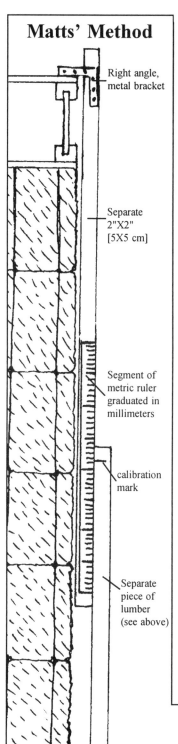

Right angle, metal bracket

Separate 2"X2" [5X5 cm]

Segment of metric ruler graduated in millimeters

calibration mark

Separate piece of lumber (see above)

studs spaced about 4' apart, would still provide a good sound barrier and pleasantly thick walls.

We do know of one building (see below), where a standard bale wall, with doorways in it, was used as a loadbearing substitute for a ridge-beam.

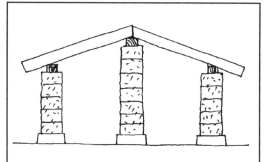

• **Compressed strawboard**. The board typically used for partitions is 2-1/4" [5.7 cm] thick and consists of compressed straw panels with paper glued onto both faces. This type of board has been widely used in England, and elsewhere, to replace sheetrock-covered frame walls. For information on PGB (Pacific Gold Board), contact BioFab, in northern California, at (916) 243-4032 or <info@strawboard.com>. If enough demand develops, a similar product will be manufactured in Texas by Agriboard. Contact them at (515) 472-0363 or <agriboard@lisco.com>.

• **Beverage cans and/or bottles** laid up in earth- or cement-based mortar (see Reynolds 1990).

Steve's Method

Generic tape measure

Measuring Compression Progress

Attaching Partition Walls to Bale Walls

Under certain circumstances (e.g., in areas with minimal seismic risk) and with certain wall types (e.g., frame walls), attachment at the top and bottom of the wall may be judged sufficient. Typically, however, partition walls are attached to exterior bale walls. The technique chosen in a particular case will depend largely on the material(s) used in building the partition wall.

Some options, arranged by partition type, are shown below. Many can also be used (although some adaptation may be needed) to connect the walls of a straw-bale addition to a preexisting structure.

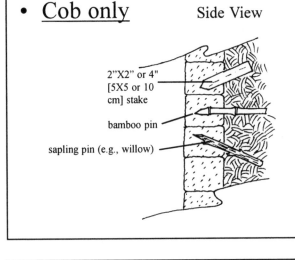

- **Cob only**   Side View

2"X2" or 4" [5X5 or 10 cm] stake

bamboo pin

sapling pin (e.g., willow)

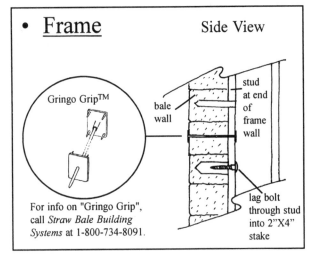

- **Frame**   Side View

Gringo Grip™

bale wall

stud at end of frame wall

For info on "Gringo Grip", call *Straw Bale Building Systems* at 1-800-734-8091.

lag bolt through stud into 2"X4" stake

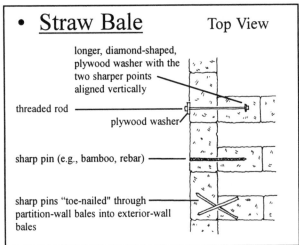

- **Straw Bale**   Top View

longer, diamond-shaped, plywood washer with the two sharper points aligned vertically

threaded rod

plywood washer

sharp pin (e.g., bamboo, rebar)

sharp pins "toe-nailed" through partition-wall bales into exterior-wall bales

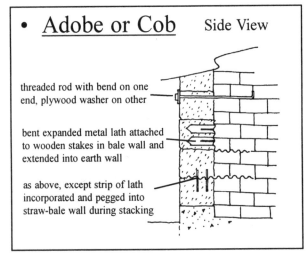

- **Adobe or Cob**   Side View

threaded rod with bend on one end, plywood washer on other

bent expanded metal lath attached to wooden stakes in bale wall and extended into earth wall

as above, except strip of lath incorporated and pegged into straw-bale wall during stacking

Not illustrated, is the technique of building the straw-bale partition wall and exterior bale wall simultaneously, knitting the two together by having some of the bales in the partition wall extend into the exterior wall. Model it with dominoes, or the equivalent, before doing it!

Insulating Floors

Under Slabs

- foamboard (of a type that can withstand the loading without compressing)
- pumice (provides an R-value of about 2.2 per inch [RSI-value of 15.2 per meter])

• Bales*

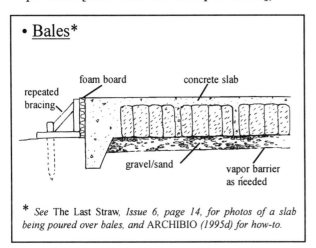

repeated bracing

foam board

concrete slab

gravel/sand

vapor barrier as needed

* See The Last Straw, Issue 6, page 14, for photos of a slab being poured over bales, and ARCHIBIO (1995d) for how-to.

Between Floor Joists/Supports

- fiberglass
- cotton
- cellulose, especially dense-packed
- integral insulation and structural floor (described, with access information for a panel with a strawboard core, on page 80).

• Bales or flakes between raised joists

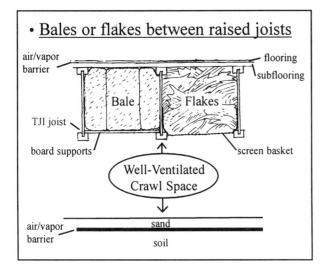

air/vapor barrier

flooring

subflooring

Bale

Flakes

TJI joist

board supports

screen basket

Well-Ventilated Crawl Space

air/vapor barrier

sand

soil

• Bales on gravel between supports

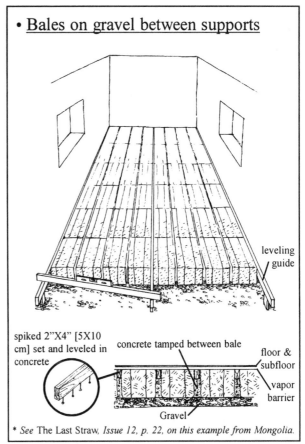

leveling guide

spiked 2"X4" [5X10 cm] set and leveled in concrete

concrete tamped between bale

floor & subfloor

vapor barrier

Gravel

* See The Last Straw, Issue 12, p. 22, on this example from Mongolia.

A wet ground surface under a raised floor may contribute to "rising damp" (water vapor in outside air) that could condense within, and lower the R/RSI-value of, the suspended insulation. Strategies to prevent this include providing as much ventilation as possible for the "crawl space" and covering the ground under the building with a layer of plastic sheeting, held down and protected by a layer of sand. Good perimeter drainage is also needed to insure that the sand stays dry.

In cold climates, warm, moist inside air must not be allowed to move downward through the floor materials. (See the diagram to the left, and CMHC 1994.) The danger lies in the possibility that the water vapor will condense, creating liquid water that will damage the floor joists and reduce the R/RSI-value of the insulation.

Step 7. Surfacing the Walls

Challenge: to provide your straw-bale walls with long-term protection, both inside and out, from the elements, the occupants, infestation by vermin and depredation by curious cattle or vandals.

Walk-Through

♣ *With the settling nearly complete, this is a good time to double-check to ensure that all gaps have been stuffed with some insulating material and, if you wish, capped with a cob mixture. Then make a final inspection of your wall surfaces. This is your last chance to do any final trimming and/or filling of gaps or depressions. Since you will soon be covering the walls, this is also your last chance to add another niche or two, more electrical boxes, more elements related to hanging things on the walls, et cetera.*

• *During the design process, decisions would have been made about how the inside and outside surfaces of the exterior walls would be surfaced. This is the last chance to reconsider those choices. A good review of the most commonly used surfacing materials is provided by Issue 9 of* The Last Straw.

The "flow chart" on page 100 takes you through the series of choices (and options) leading to a completed and maintained surface. Whether the wall surface in question is inside or outside, and whether one chooses a plaster-type surface or one of the non-plaster options, an early decision involves whether to install a barrier against air (and the water vapor it contains), or water in liquid form or both. If you elect to use a barrier, one must then decide whether it will cover the whole wall or only a portion (usually the lower part). The sidebar to the

flow chart looks at considerations related to these decisions.

If you do decide to use a plaster-type material, the next major decision involves whether to use some sort of netting as reinforcement. The choice made here has significant implications, which we explore on page 101.

However, even if you chose plaster for most of the straw-bale wall surfaces, you might still consider using drywall, attached to vertical "furring strips", on surfaces against which you plan to attach things like floor-and wall-mounted kitchen cabinets. Drywall is an inexpensive material which, when properly "furred out", will provide you with wonderfully smooth, straight surfaces to mount things against. For more details on attaching "furring strips", see page 131.

• *Issue 9 of* The Last Straw *includes an article by Jon Ruez (1995) that provides field-tested, detailed information about attaching reinforcement to a straw-bale building. Please note, however, that Jon would now recommend attaching the stucco netting after the expanded metal lath is in place, rather than before. Use Jon's article as a general guide. When it comes to specifics, use his suggestions, those in this and other books and videos, and those gleaned from conversations with other bale builders. Weigh the options in light of your unique situation, and then choose the materials/techniques that are right for you.*

♣ *For our "model" building, we can now wrap the building's corners with <u>galvanized</u>, expanded metal lath (a.k.a. "diamond lath" and "blood lath"), to reinforce the plaster at these often-bumped locations. The same type of reinforcement is recommended at door and window openings. First, as appropriate, protect the edge of the wooden frame with a waterproof material (see below for options). Then attach one edge of an appropriately shaped piece of lath to one edge of the frame. Finally, wrap this piece out onto the wall and secure it with "Roberta" pins (see page 92).*

As part of this process, some builders add a commercially available metal edging strip, called "J-strip", to provide a uniform way to eventually end the plaster against the door and window frames (see diagram at bottom of page). At such openings, many builders take great pains to create corner coverage with no gaps, in hopes of preventing the diagonal cracks that so typically appear in the plaster at these locations. Additional resistance can be provided by attaching an extra strip of lath near each corner as shown in diagram, upper right.

The cut edges of this lath are like many, tiny razor blades *(therefore, "blood lath"). Gloves are highly recommended.*

♣ *On the outside of the wall, cover all exposed metal and wood with roofing felt or some other waterproof material to isolate them from the damp plaster. A thinner,*

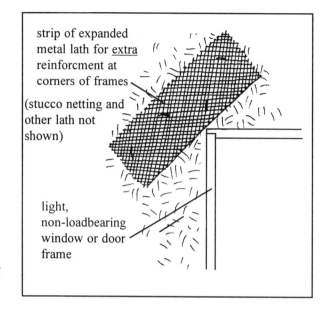

strip of expanded metal lath for <u>extra</u> reinforcment at corners of frames

(stucco netting and other lath not shown)

light, non-loadbearing window or door frame

commonly used alternative to roofing felt is Plaster Kraft Paper (a.k.a. Kraft paper, Grade D paper, or black paper). You may also want (or be required) to protect external, RBA tie-downs from any contact with plaster-type materials by covering them with strips of roofing felt or the equivalent. This will protect them against rusting and corrosion. It may also, as described later in this "walk-through", allow the tie-downs to be retightened after the first coat of plaster has hardened. Expanded metal lath is needed over these waterproof materials to hold the first coat of plaster in place until it cures, and to provide additional reinforcement where the plaster is not keyed into the bale surface.

Expanded Metal Lath Meets Wood Frame

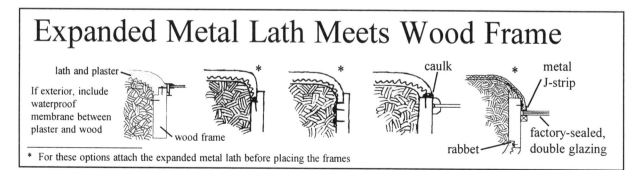

lath and plaster

If exterior, include waterproof membrane between plaster and wood

wood frame

*

*

caulk

rabbet

*

metal J-strip

factory-sealed, double glazing

* For these options attach the expanded metal lath before placing the frames

♣ *For our "model" building, we can now continue the process of surfacing the walls by creating an exterior curtain of stucco netting, securely attached at the top to the RBA and at the bottom to the wooden "nailer" in the side of the grade-beam collar. The toe-up system involving pressure-treated 2"X4"s [5X10 cm] fastened to a slab (see the diagram on page 47) also provides a convenient nailer both outside and in. One-inch mesh poultry netting (a.k.a. "chicken wire") is commonly used as a substitute for stucco netting, but may not meet code.*

• **For both expanded metal lath and stucco netting, the orientation of the openings in the material is important only where they are placed against something other than straw (e.g., roofing felt or a "barrier" material).** *For metal lath, in such cases, the longer dimension of the diamond-shaped openings should run horizontally and the narrow strips of metal that form the mesh should slope downward <u>toward</u> the wall. For stucco netting applied over something other than straw, the long dimension of the "diamonds should also be horizontal. In addition, the small, slightly protruding sections of wire, designed to hold the netting away from the underlying material, should be on the inside. When used directly over straw, both materials can be used in any orientation you find most convenient. The crucial thing is that the plaster be applied with enough force to leave the lath or netting completely imbedded in the plaster.*

So, when wrapping the outside corners of a building with "blood lath", we can use a single, full-width strip run vertically. Ah, but what if some or all of the courses are covered with a barrier to exclude liquid water? In such a case, you may also want to use stucco netting (or an equivalent). This, combined with the "improperly" oriented lath, will adequately support the first coat of plaster until it hardens.

Focusing now on stucco netting, imagine a design in which only the first course of bales has a waterproof drape. **Which way do we want to orient the strips of netting?** *Straw-bale builders have usually chosen the* **horizontal orientation**, *perhaps having seen it used this way in mainstream construction. Those building in earthquake-prone areas might be acting on the hunch that wrapping corners with horizontal strips may provide stronger reinforcement at these critical locations than a series of vertical strips connected at a limited number of points along their overlap. Many builders, if orienting the strips horizontally, chose to initially run them right across door and window openings, coming back later to custom cut and make attachments to the frames.*

The **vertical orientation**, *although generally less used so far, seems to have some advantages. A series of strips of equal length can be precut. Given their restricted length and secure attachment to the non-movable RBA, the strips can more easily be pulled taut before the lower end is fastened to the toe-up or the foundation. This removes much of the looseness that would otherwise have to be dealt with as described on the next page. Another possible advantage is that, instead of having to move back and forth along horizontal strips, one can do all the work on each strip from the same general location. This can mean a lot less moving of scaffolding and/or ladders. One case in which you <u>must</u> use the vertical orientation is when you are using the netting as a tie-down system after you have pre-stressed the walls (as described on page 73).*

Considering the way doors and windows

interrupt stretches of wall surface, the most efficient approach might be to use vertical strips in the unbroken areas, while using horizontal strips to fill in the gaps above and below frames.

♣ *Regardless of your of choice of orientation, or whether you use both, you should connect the strips of netting where you have purposely overlapped them by a minimum of two inches [about 10 cm]. One time-honored technique involves binding selected pairs of wires (one from each strip, for greatest effect) together with wire twists or "cage clips" (small, "C"-shaped pieces of galvanized wire). To easily hold and pinch the latter shut, you'll need to buy a special pair of pliers, shown below, or modify a pair of needle nose pliers that you already have by grinding small, cupped grooves near each tip.*

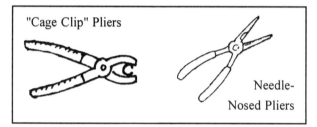

"Cage Clip" Pliers

Needle-Nosed Pliers

♣ *With the curtain of stucco netting now complete, we can secure it to the bale wall with galvanized wire pushed through the wall with a "bale needle". The diagram on page 102 shows several options. One or two ties per bale is typical, although in very small buildings they have been successfully omitted entirely. Again, only you know how much insurance you want, while guessing at how much insurance any given expenditure of time/labor/money will actually provide. Since our "model" building will have earth plaster, without reinforcement, on the inside surfaces, there will be nothing to which we could fasten the inside end of a wire tie. One option is to fasten one end securely at the midpoint of a*

short piece of rebar, bamboo, etc., and then push the free end through the wall from the inside to the outside. The loose end can then be twisted around the netting, securing it to the wall.

Springy areas between these through-ties can be snugged to the bales with long, narrow wire staples (often called "Robert or Roberta pins" to emphasize their size and status relative to "bobby pins"). Square-end "jute net staples", used to hold down erosion control netting, can be purchased as an alternative.

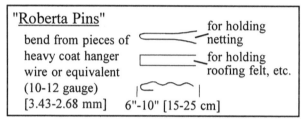

"Roberta Pins"
bend from pieces of
heavy coat hanger
wire or equivalent
(10-12 gauge)
[3.43-2.68 mm]

for holding netting
for holding roofing felt, etc.
6"-10" [15-25 cm]

Pronounced springiness/looseness can be dealt with by shortening selected wires in the netting. The low-tech method involves grabbing a wire with a pair of "needle nosed" pliers and twisting. Tim Farrant and John Watt, faced with the daunting task of tightening netting on many hundreds of linear feet of privacy wall in Tucson, came up with a high-tech method that saved time and spared their wrists. As shown below, it uses a homemade, slotted device mounted in a clutch-equipped, battery-operated "screw gun". Slip the tool onto a wire, pull the trigger, pull the tool out of the twist, and proceed to the next location. Enough to make a Luddite twist in her grave, eh?

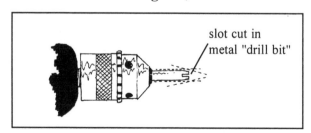

slot cut in metal "drill bit"

♣ Before you lose the opportunity, create one or more "truth windows" on interior (and/or exterior) to provide skeptics with irrefutable evidence that your building really is made of bales. Glass or Plexiglas in a frame works well, as do small, salvaged windows. Consider covering interior "truth windows" with art work in a side-hinged frame.

♣ In our model building, cement-based, exterior plaster can now be hand-applied, or blown on by a pumper rig (see page 107). Typically, three coats are applied, with the final, thin "color" coat containing a pigment.

Blowing a thick, initial coat of plaster onto a wall adds a great deal of weight quickly, and produces some additional compression. This will, in turn, loosen the tie-downs you have so carefully created to hold down the RBA and roof. Not to worry. If you have used the in-the-wall system with threaded rods (and purposely not blocked off access to the nuts), simply tighten them up one last time, after the initial coat has hardened. If you have used an external tie-down system (e.g., polyester strapping), and have prevented the plaster from contacting the tie-downs _and_ have left uncovered the hardware for tightening them, you can now attempt to tighten them one last time. The other, more common, approach is to simply let well enough alone. This leaves the slightly loosened tie-downs to act as a backup. They will function only in the very unlikely case that the weight of the plaster and bale "sandwich" is not enough to resist the uplift created by the Hurricane from Hell.

To achieve maximum strength, each coat of any cement-based plaster must be kept moist until fully cured (about 48 hours). Without this extra moisture, the chemical reaction which hardens the plaster cannot be completed.

Although the "model" building being tracked here has mud plaster only on the interior walls, both stabilized (i.e., water-resistant) and natural mud plasters have been successfully used on the exterior walls of straw-bale walls (the latter needing ample roof overhangs in wetter climates).

♣ The plans for the building call for un-stabilized mud plaster applied directly to the straw, on the interior surfaces of the straw-bale walls. There will be no stucco netting, but you will still need to attach expanded metal lath over any metal or wood that will be covered by the plaster. Although the building code may not require covering metal or wood within the building with roofing felt, or the equivalent, some builders do it anyway. The rationale for covering metal is that the rust on ungalvanized metals may bleed through and discolor the interior plaster. For wood, the rationale is this—the more you can isolate the wood from water in any form, the less it will undergo cycles of shrinking and swelling that, in turn, can stress the plaster, eventually causing cracks.

♣ The earthen (a.k.a. adobe or mud) plaster can now be applied directly onto the bales with a trowel or your hand, taking care to press the mud firmly into all depressions, cracks and crannies. Typically, two or three layers are applied, the last often being a clay slip that provides a surface that is uniform in both smoothness and color. The use of such slips as a decorative technique is covered on page 116. An excellent resource for earthen plasters is Steen and Steen (1997a).

Plasters 101 — The Basics

Hang around the straw-bale revival for a while, and you're bound to hear the bewildering jargon related to surfacing materials. The name used by a manufacturer's technical support person for some material/tool/item-of-hardware, may differ from the name used by the local salesman or tradeswoman, which may, in turn, differ from the name your grandmother taught you. In a different part of the country, someone's grandmother will teach them an entirely different name. It gets even more confusing when you run into things like Keene's Cement—it isn't cement at all, but rather a type of gypsum used in some interior plaster "recipes".

The English have a great, catchall word—render—which comfortably includes a wide variety of mixtures that one might "smear" on a wall to protect it. However, since we, in the U.S. of A., don't really speak English, that isn't much help. The best we can do for a catchall is "plaster", so we'll start off by defining that.

Plaster is a combination of materials which, when mixed with a suitable amount of water (sometimes containing dissolved ingredients), forms a plastic mass which, when applied to a surface, adheres to it and subsequently "sets up" or hardens. The noun "coat", when used in reference to plaster, means an individual thickness, or layer, of plaster applied to a wall surface. With very rare exceptions, two or more coats are used, being numbered consecutively from the inner surface to the outer. For a traditional three-coat plaster application, the first coat is called the "scratch" coat, because it is typically scratched to create horizontal grooves. In straw-bale construction, it is generally applied in a thickness adequate to fully cover the straw and to encompass the

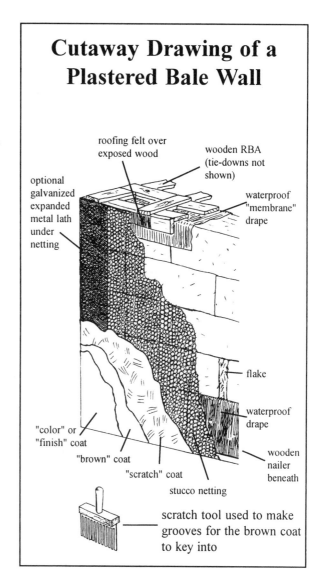

Cutaway Drawing of a Plastered Bale Wall

roofing felt over exposed wood

wooden RBA (tie-downs not shown)

optional galvanized expanded metal lath under netting

waterproof "membrane" drape

flake

waterproof drape

"color" or "finish" coat

wooden nailer beneath

"brown" coat

"scratch" coat

stucco netting

scratch tool used to make grooves for the brown coat to key into

wire reinforcement (if any). The attachment of the second, or "brown" coat, is increased by the plaster keying into the grooves in the "scratch" coat. The 'brown" coat, which is typically no less than ¼ inch [about 6 mm] thick, provides a smooth, flat surface onto which the the third, thinner [about 1/8" or 3 mm] "finish" or "color" coat is applied. Lumped together, the first two coats are often referred to as the "base coat".

It is characteristic of plaster mixes that they contain two sorts of ingredients. The **aggregate**, usually sand, or a lightweight aggregate (e.g., pumice, perlite, vermiculite), provides most of the volume. The **binder(s)**, primarily occupying the spaces between the particles of aggregate, acts as the "glue". By themselves, the "binders" tend to shrink and crack as they cure and/or dry. An important role of the "aggregate" is to reduce or eliminate this cracking, thus preserving the strength and integrity of the hardened plaster. Since the binder(s), more than the aggregate, generally determines the nature and usage of a plaster, it makes sense to categorize plasters by their dominant binder.

Less often, plasters will contain an **admixture**. The term refers to anything, other than aggregate and binder, that is included to modify the plaster mixture in some beneficial way. Two common examples are chopped glass-fibers (for cement-based plasters) and emulsified asphalt (a waterproofer for earthen plasters).

• **Cement-based plasters** are very commonly used on bale buildings for both exterior and (less often) interior surfacing. They generally consist primarily of cement and sand, usually in a ratio of about one part cement (or, cement and lime) to about three to four parts of sand. The lime acts primarily as a "plasticizer", increasing the workability of the plaster. A common, modern addition to the "scratch" and "brown" coats, is small amounts of ½ inch [1.25 cm] long fibers of alkali resistant materials (e.g., polypropylene, glass). By increasing the tensile strength and reducing the shrinkage of the plaster, they (arguably) reduce cracking. When applied to exterior surfaces, cement- based plaster is commonly referred to as "stucco", although in some areas this term refers only to factory-prepared, finish-coat mixtures.

Cement (the binder in these plasters) is not a naturally occurring material. It is usually made by creating a carefully formulated mixture of finely ground limestone, clay, alumina and other naturally occurring mineral materials, and then heating this mixture to high temperatures in large rotating kilns. The resulting balls of "clinker" are then ground up along with a small amount of uncalcined gypsum (which retards the eventual hardening process) to create a powdery material. This powder (which we call cement), when mixed with water and kept moist during the "curing" process, changes chemically and becomes a hard mass.

The mining, transportation, grinding and "burning" required to create cement results in a high "embodied energy" (i.e., it takes a lot of fossil fuel energy to produce it). For this reason, many thoughtful builders use less energy-intensive substitutes where possible. Another disadvantage of cement, when wet, is its somewhat caustic nature. You'll be wise to follow the manufacturers advice regarding its safe use.

Cement does, however, have some attractive properties for use as a binder:

—It is available virtually anywhere.

—There are good written resources (especially, Melander and Isberner 1996) and (often) good, local human resources to help the novice learn its proper use.

—Standard "recipes" are possible, since a given type of cement (e.g., Portland Type I) is the same wherever it's made.

—It produces a plaster that bonds well to straw, is resistant to scratching (i.e., hard), has considerable compressive and shear strength, is seldom affected by repeated freeze/thaw cycles and is unaffected by water.

• **Lime-based plasters** have been used for centuries for both exterior and interior surfacing, and are being used by a small, but growing, number of straw-bale practitioners, mostly for exterior surfacing. Lime is made by "burning" (a.k.a. calcining) limestone (calcium carbonate) . Carbon dioxide gas is driven off, leaving calcium oxide, which we call lime or, more accurately, quicklime. Since quicklime is extremely caustic, it is soaked in water (i.e., slaked), which converts it to hydrated lime (calcium hydroxide). Although much less caustic than quicklime, **bags of hydrated lime do carry cautionary warnings regarding its safe use. Play it safe!**

To further complicate things, hydrated lime comes in two types—S and N. In your area, either one or both types may be available without special order. Having consulted producers, users, and an authority on historical plastering technology, we are convinced that both types can be successfully used as a binder. If an aged, lime putty (see below) is <u>not</u> being used, Type S may be the better choice because it develops plasticity more quickly. Type N, on the other hand, develops its strength more rapidly and may bond more firmly to earthen substrates.

When used in plasters, lime of either type is often soaked in water to form a lime putty. The longer you can soak it, the more "plastic" it will be (we've read that Roman law forbade the use of lime putty less than three years old). When a lime/sand plaster is applied to a wall, the lime begins to slowly change <u>chemically</u>, hardening as it absorbs carbon dioxide and/or carbonic acid gas from the air. For this reason, lime-based plasters were traditionally applied in several thin, successive coats. This provided the material in each coat with more exposure to the atmosphere, and

thus with more opportunity to harden.

Despite lime having an embodied energy slightly higher than cement, lime-based plasters offer several possible advantages to the straw-builder. Due to their excellent plasticity, they can be applied without wire reinforcement, although substitutes (e.g., burlap fabric) have occasionally been used. If kept wet, a mix that contains <u>only</u> lime and sand can be stored indefinitely. Lime-based plasters are reputedly much more "breathable" (i.e., more permeable to air and any water vapor in it) than their cement-based counterparts. Finally, micro-cracks in the plaster can be "healed", over time, by deposition of new lime in the crack. Other than the material provided herein, and the booklet published by the Canello Project (Steen and Steen 1997a), there are unfortunately no readily available, modern, written resources providing detailed information about lime-based plasters.

• **Gypsum-based plasters** are used exclusively on interior surfaces because they are subject to deterioration if exposed to water. The naturally occurring mineral called gypsum is hydrous calcium sulfate (i.e., there are attached water molecules). When this form of gypsum is heated (i.e., calcined), most of this water is driven off. The entire process of creating calcined gypsum gives it an embodied energy that is only about one-third that of cement.

When calcined gypsum is mixed with water, it recombines with it, changing <u>chemically</u> and reverting quickly to its hard, crystalline form. We are most familiar with it as the primary ingredient in quick setting "plaster of Paris". When mixed with additives that delay the rate at which it hardens, it can be a useful binder for interior plasters.

Gypsum is usually purchased with the retardants already added. To increase the hardness of finish coat mixes, lime is often included as an additive. Helpful information about commercially available gypsum-based products is often available from the manufacturers (e.g., U. S. Gypsum). Also, check the bag that a product comes in for instructions regarding its proper use. If you want to create relatively hard, extremely smooth interior surfaces, gypsum plasters are the way to go. Be advised, however, that because they generally harden (i.e., set) quickly and require skillful trowel work, you may want to practice in closets, or the like, before tackling more visible surfaces.

• **Clay-based (a.k.a. earthen, adobe, mud) plasters** depend on very small, disc-shaped clay particles, present in many soils, to bind together the larger silt- and sand-sized particles. Particularly in drier regions, they have been used to surface both the interior and exterior of straw-bale buildings. The "binding" properties of clay result <u>not</u> from any chemical reaction with water, but from the adhesion of the platelike clay particles to each other during the <u>drying</u> process that hardens the plaster. Liquid water, when placed in contact with dry, clay-based plaster, is drawn back into the spaces between the platelets of clay, softening the plaster and making it subject to erosion.

The erodability of typical earthen plasters presents a problem in all but very dry climates, unless the walls are protected by large roof overhangs (which often function also as porches). Strategies for reducing the erodability usually involve adding various substances to the plaster itself. Some depend on their <u>physical form</u>, as in the case of chopped straw in mud plaster. To work most effectively, the plaster must be applied in

strokes that end with the hand or tool moving horizontally. This leaves the short straws oriented horizontally in the plaster, such that they repeatedly interrupt the flow of water down the wall. Acting as miniature "check dams", they prevent the formation of concentrated rivulets and reduce the erosive power of the water (see Crocker, 1995).

Other additives depend on <u>chemical</u> properties. This include a wide variety of substances ranging from high-tech (e.g., soil stabilizing chemicals and enzymes) to mid-tech (e.g., emulsified asphalt) to low-tech (e.g., exterior grade glue, animal dung). They are usually distributed throughout the plaster, although some have been applied to the dried finish coat as a sealer.

Another minor problem experienced by people using clay-based plasters on interior surfaces is "dusting". This is the tendency for small particles to separate from the surface and fall to the floor, or to rub off on your tuxedo (too much champagne?). For details regarding erodability and dusting, see pages 113-114 and 116, respectively.

Given the above-mentioned problems, why would anyone want to use an earthen plaster? A partial list of reasons, ranging from ecological to esthetic, is provided below.

—The acquisition of clay-rich soils, unless done on a commercial basis, generally leaves scars that are small and (often) temporary. This is usually not true for the other binders.

—Earth plasters can have a very low price tag. Some lucky builders have been able to use the soil from their foundation excavation, perhaps with a little sand added, leaving no scar at all. Fortunately, for those not so lucky, soils with sufficient clay content to bind the plaster can generally be found within a reasonable distance. Even then, however, samples from a number of sources may have to be experimented with before a satisfactory mix is developed (see page 113).

—Since earthen plasters are usually applied directly to the bales without the use of stucco netting or any substitute, an expensive, labor-intensive step is avoided.

—Mud plasters are more "user-friendly" than the alternatives. The application of mud plaster is easier, especially for the novice plasterer, since a good mix has both sufficient plasticity and excellent adherence to the bale surface. Cleanup of tools and mixing equipment, although more easily done when the residue is still wet, can be done long after an earthen plaster has dried and hardened. With gypsum- and cement-based plasters (and to a lesser extent with lime-based and asphalt-stabilized earthen plasters), one is well advised to do thorough cleanup prior to any pause long enough to allow the plaster to "set up". Since clay-based plasters, even if stabilized with asphalt emulsion, harden only as a result of drying, partially-used batches can be preserved indefinitely for future use simply by keeping the mix wet.

—When earthen plasters are applied without the use of woven wire netting for reinforcement, the integrity of the plaster depends on its attachment to the straw. As opposed to cement-based plaster, it cannot become a disconnected "curtain", hanging from the RBA and hiding water damage that may be taking place behind it. If not firmly attached to "healthy" straw, mud plaster is likely to soon end up on the ground. Not a pretty sight, but better to learn of problems earlier than later.

—And, speaking of pretty sights, it's hard to beat the look and feel of a softly irregular, subtly variegated, earth-plastered wall. Earth not only feels right as a covering for a material that emerged from the earth, but it

also feels right to your fingers, or against your cheek—firm but not harsh, inanimate but not dead. MUD, GLORIOUS MUD!

Although our way of grouping the plasters may suggest that each can contain only one binder, many mixes contain several. Cement-based plasters usually also contain lime, which functions there not as a binder, but as an agent to make the wet mix stickier and easier to apply. Lime-based plasters often contain a small amount of cement as an additional, quick-to-harden binder. Although cement appears not to work well, generally, as an additional binder in earthen plasters, a small amount of lime seems to improve their strength (DESIGNER/builder 1996).

Photo by Judy Knox

Don't let a pig do your plastering!

Plasters at a Glance (a very subjective ranking)

The ranking symbols are 2×2 boxes filled from empty (worst) to solid black (best). Below, each cell is described by its fill level: **full** = solid black (best, greatest); **empty** = open grid (worst, least); intermediate values are given as fractions.

Criteria / Property / Characteristic \ Type of Plaster	Cement-based	Lime-based	Gypsum-based, Interior Use Only	Clay-based, Natural	Clay-based, Asphalt-stabilized
low embodied energy in binder	¼	¼	½	full	full
chemically benign binder (non-caustic)	½	empty	½	full	full
availability of binder or pre-packaged mix	full	full	full	empty to full	empty to full
workability (good cohesion and adhesion)	½	½	½	full	full
likelihood of success on straw bales without reinforcement	½	½	½	full	full
resistance to erosion by water	full	¾	½	empty	½
rapid development of strength	½	empty	full	½	½
eventual hardness	full	½	full	½	½
breathability	empty	full	½	full	full
low maintenance	½	½	full	empty	½
no moist curing needed	empty	full	full	full	full
friendliness to novices, overall	½	½	½	full	¾

■ = best, greatest   ⊞ = worst, least

Air & Moisture Barriers

Purpose – to prevent the movement of air (and water vapor), and/or the diffusion of water vapor, and/or the passage of liquid water into the bale walls.

Common Barrier Materials – polyethylene plastic sheeting (barrier to air, water vapor, and water), vapor barrier paints (used as a barrier to water vapor), breathable "house wraps" (barrier to air and water).

Possible Placement – Depending on the strategy, barriers may be placed on the interior surface, on the exterior surface or, occasionally, on both. Breathable "housewraps" are generally used only on the outside surface, and generally only on the lowest courses.

Pros and Cons – Generally not recommended in temperate climates, since they prevent the plaster from "keying" into the roughness of the bales and reduce the wall's ability to "breath". In climates with simultaneous wind and rain or drifting snow, a curtain of "housewrap material" extending part way up the outside of the wall should be considered. In colder climates, air/vapor barriers may be needed on the interior surfaces to prevent water vapor from moving into the wall and condensing. Their use may dictate using a mechanical air exchanger to maintain acceptable indoor air quality. See Gibson (1994) and Lstiburek and Carmody (1993) for more detail.

Flow Chart for Wall-Surfacing Decision-Making

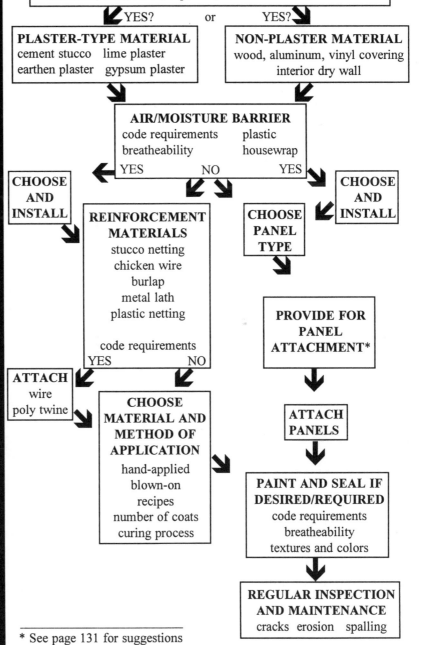

SURFACING BALE WALLS

Considerations: climate, long-term maintenance, desired appearance, interior or exterior surface, cost, embodied energy, resources, time, labor, expertise, assistance from others.

YES? or YES?

PLASTER-TYPE MATERIAL
cement stucco   lime plaster
earthen plaster gypsum plaster

NON-PLASTER MATERIAL
wood, aluminum, vinyl covering
interior dry wall

AIR/MOISTURE BARRIER
code requirements   plastic
breatheability   housewrap
YES   NO   YES

CHOOSE AND INSTALL

REINFORCEMENT MATERIALS
stucco netting
chicken wire
burlap
metal lath
plastic netting

code requirements
YES   NO

CHOOSE PANEL TYPE

CHOOSE AND INSTALL

PROVIDE FOR PANEL ATTACHMENT*

ATTACH
wire
poly twine

CHOOSE MATERIAL AND METHOD OF APPLICATION
hand-applied
blown-on
recipes
number of coats
curing process

ATTACH PANELS

PAINT AND SEAL IF DESIRED/REQUIRED
code requirements
breatheability
textures and colors

REGULAR INSPECTION AND MAINTENANCE
cracks erosion spalling

* See page 131 for suggestions regarding panel attachment.

Reinforcement for Plaster

Purpose—It helps to hold the "scratch" coat in place, reduce cracking, tie down the roof plate, sandwich the walls for increased resistance to dislocation by seismic forces, and satisfy code requirements.

Types—The most common types are 1" [2.5 cm] poultry netting, stucco netting (heavier wire than in chicken netting), and galvanized expanded metal lath (a.k.a. diamond lath). Plastic mesh or natural fabic/netting may provide an alternative for those reluctant to use metal netting. In a number of buildings, lime/sand plaster has been applied onto burlap fabric previously attached to the bales and to door and window frames.

Pros and Cons - Many builders use expanded metal lath: 1) where plaster butts up against or covers roofing felt, metal or wood; 2) where interior and exterior wall surfaces curve in at door and window openings; 3) on all outside wall corners.

Covering both surfaces of the bale walls with netting of any kind has considerable costs in time, labor, money and resources. If you plan to use reinforcement in your plaster,

build adequate time into the work schedule for the labor-intensive process of attaching it to the walls. If you believe that interference with Earth's natural electromagnetic fields can adversely affect human health, add that as an additional cost of using wire netting (see Pinsky 1995).

You will have to decide, in your particular situation just how much "insurance" you want, and how much you're willing to pay for it. Both cement- and clay-based plasters have been used successfully on bale walls without the benefit of reinforcement. The track record, however, is still being established. The likelihood of success without reinforcement will be enhanced if the plaster is applied to the "cut" edge of the bales, rather than the "folded" edge. Since bales come with one of each, some builders have used a chainsaw to trim about a half inch [1.25 cm] off the folded edge of each bale before stacking them, thus creating bales with two cut edges. Other builders have settled for stacking the bales such that every other bale in each course has the cut edge exposed.

Photo by Hesh Fisk

The Little Taj (a.k.a. Mom's Place) ready for plastering. Note expanded metal lath at corner and black paper over wood and metal.

Photo by Hesh Fisk

Note 2" x 4" ledgers for hanging cabinets, and seat built into load bearing window frame. Angled opening created with carpentry.

Attaching the Plaster Reinforcement

Polypropylene baling twine has occasionally been used for through-ties. However, galvanized wire is much more commonly used, with 16 gauge [1.59 mm] being typical. A good alternative is the slightly lighter, 17 gauge [1.37 mm] wire used on electric fences. It comes wound on metal spools that can be belt-mounted for convenient dispensing.

In situations where there will be periodic inspections by a building official, you may be required to use some specific type of reinforcement netting (or mesh), and may have to attach it in very specific ways. Some options for attaching stucco netting with through-ties are shown below. Do your homework so that you get it "right" the first time. If you are building "without benefit" of inspections, and the structure is small and the likelihood of earthquakes is even smaller, you do have the option of dispensing with the through-ties altogether. Again, what level of "insurance" are you comfortable with?

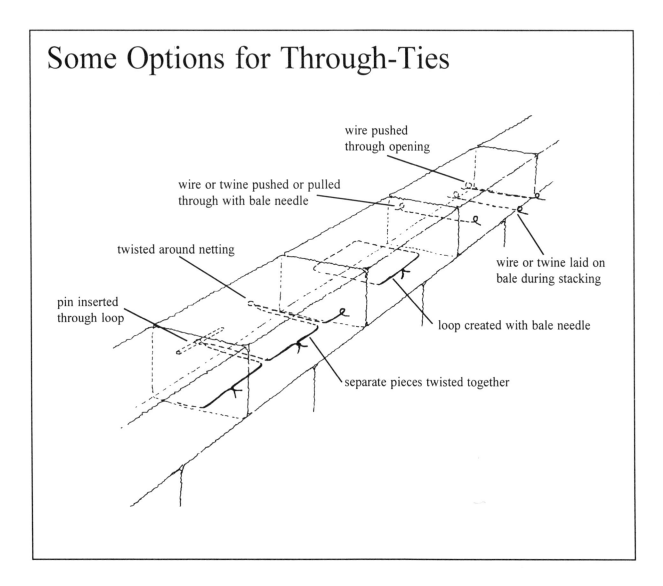

Some Options for Through-Ties

wire pushed through opening

wire or twine pushed or pulled through with bale needle

twisted around netting

wire or twine laid on bale during stacking

pin inserted through loop

loop created with bale needle

separate pieces twisted together

Plasters 201 — (some of) The Details

This section contains, for each of our four binders, selected information on "recipes", mixing, application, curing/drying, decorating and, where appropriate, sealing. Please note that for each type of plaster, as with potato salad, every veteran practitioner has their favorite recipe. Many differ only slightly from each other, and produce results so similar that even their "owners" can't tell them apart. We have gathered together, from sources ranging from hard bound to hide-bound, a collection that we hope is generally representative of what people are actually using. For additional options, more specialized or exotic, consult Issue 9 of *The Last Straw*, *Plastering Skills* (Van Den Branden and Hartsell 1984), *The Earthbuilder's Encyclopedia* (Tibbets 1989), *Earth Construction* (Houlen and Guillard 1994), *The Straw Bale House Book* (Steen et al. 1994), and *Earthen and Lime Plasters* (Steen and Steen 1997a).

As usual, we welcome your suggestions for "recipes" you think should be included in the next (Goddess forbid!) version of this opus. All of our recipes use "parts by volume" unless otherwise indicated.

Cement-Based Plasters

Recipes

The Old Standby
This mix can be used for all three coats:
- 1 part cement
- 1 part lime, Type S (if available).
- 5 to 8 parts clean plaster sand (a mix with five parts sand will—arguably—be harder, more expensive per unit volume, and less breathable)

Pumper Mix
This is a recipe regularly used on straw-bale walls by Tucson-based Hansen Kramer Stuccoing, Inc. They mix in large batches and blow the plaster on with a "stucco pump". The bags of cement they use weigh 94 pounds [42.7 kilos]; those of lime weigh 50 pounds [22.7 kilos]; those of silica sand weigh 100 pounds [45.5 kilos].

Scratch Coat
- 2 bags of cement
- 1 bag of lime
- 40 square-end shovels of screened clean, sand

Brown Coat
- 2 bags cement
- 1 bag lime
- 40 rounded shovels of screened, clean sand

Finish Coat
- 1 bag cement
- 2 bags lime
- 40 rounded shovels of screened clean sand (use finer silica sand for a smoother finish)

Mixing

Cement-based plasters can be successfully mixed either by hand or by machine. Hand

gasoline-powered plaster mixer

Some Tools of the Trade

mortar hoe

rounded finish trowel

brick trowel

finishing trowel

sponge trowel

Poor Man's Sifter Set-up
fine screens attached to old bed frames, leaning on stack of straw bales

mixing is usually done in a wheelbarrow or in a mixing tub/trough, store-bought or homemade. A mortar hoe (see figure above) will greatly speed up the process of thoroughly mixing all the dry ingredients until a uniform color is achieved. Only then is water added until the desired degree of stiffness/looseness is achieved.

A recommended sequence of steps for effective hand-mixing is as follows:

1) Position about half of the sand near one end of the mixing container.

2) Onto this sand, put all of the cement and lime.

3) Cover the cement and lime with the remaining sand.

4) Add any dry admixture(s) (e.g., fibers).

5) Using a mortar hoe, "chop" and pull the dry materials toward the empty end of the container. Repeat this process, switching ends as needed, until the mix acquires a uniform color.

6) With the homogeneous dry mix at one end, add some of the required water to the empty end.

7) Chop the dry mix into the water, adding more water as needed, until the desired degree of workability has been acheived.

As you approach the desired consistency, (which we could easily show you on a job site, but can't usefully describe in words), very small amounts of additional water cause great reductions in the stiffness. Toward the end, go really slowly! Too little water in the mix may result in an incomplete curing (and reduced strength) and will make it difficult to key the plaster into the roughness of the bales or the scratch coat. Too much water will make the plaster difficult to scoop up and apply with a trowel, reduce the strength of the cured plaster, and increase shrinkage (and cracking). Have a veteran show you what a "good mix" looks and acts like, then try some plastering with their mix to really get a feel for it.

Mixing by machine can make the job a whole lot easier. Concrete mixers, powered either by gasoline or electricity, can do a decent job of mixing your plaster, but a plaster (a.k.a. mortar) mixer can do better, larger batches in less time. When a batch is ready, it is usually dumped into wheelbarrows for transfer to the scene of the action. Whichever type of mixer you use, there is a preferred sequence for adding your materials:

1) Add about 90% of the required water (determined by prior experimentation).

2) Add about 50% of the required sand.

3) Add all of the lime (if any), then all of the cement, then any dry admixtures (e.g., color pigments) or fibers.

4) Add the remaining sand.

5) Mix, adding the remaining water only as needed, until the batch is uniform in color and of the desired consistency.

RED

Cement is formulated to provide adequate time for placement and necessary manipulation of the plaster before it begins to harden. If you mix too big a batch, however, it may begin to harden while still in the wheelbarrow. The hardening process, in this case, cannot be interrupted by covering the mix with plastic sheeting or be reversed by adding more water. Get the stuff out of the wheelbarrow and off your tools, and make a note to adjust the size of the batch to the rate at which it can be applied with the available equipment and work force.

Application

Cement-based plasters are applied either by hand or with aid of some sort of mechanical equipment, either human-powered or otherwise. The only performance advantage

that machine applied plaster may have over the hand applied version, is that the scratch coat will probably be more fully keyed into the roughness of the bale-wall surface. Some owner-builder's have the first coat blown on by a plastering contractor, letting them do the heavy work and getting the wall protected quickly. Then, at their own pace, they (and friends!) can do the other coat(s).

Hand application, especially for the scratch coat, could mean just that—a human hand in a rubber glove. Most novice plasterers can exert much more pressure, to push plaster into the roughness of the bale surface with the heel of their hand than with a trowel. And, for them, it may be just as fast. **However, be sure that all the cut ends of wires are tucked away where they cannot jab the unsuspecting plasterer**.

RED

The traditional system, however, involves the use of a **"mortarboard", a "hawk" and a trowel** (see diagram to the left). The plaster is first shoveled onto the "mortarboard", a flat piece of water-saturated or nonabsorbent material placed near the plasterer (often elevated to facilitate use of the trowel to transfer plaster from it to the "hawk"). With several trowel-loads of plaster now on the "hawk", the next step involves getting some plaster onto the trowel, and then onto the wall (see diagram to the left). In the Portland Cement Association's excellent publication (Melander and Isberner,1996), they make the process sound very easy. We quote, "After transferring some of the plaster from the hawk to the trowel, the plasterer lays the plaster on the surface." For a novice, the reality is more likely to be, "While attempting, with an awkward tool called a trowel, to pick up some of the plaster from the demoniacally heavy, plaster-loaded hawk, the frustrated plasterer lays most of the plaster on his or her feet,

Cutting From a Hawk

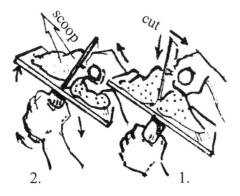

scoop

cut

2.   1.

"It's tricky. You'll drop a lot before you learn. The secret is a certain twist of the hand and wrist, while tilting the hawk with a little motion...The motion of plastering is more like a sweep or arc, while using a pressure...Keep the hawk about one foot from the wall. It will be hard to keep plaster from falling off the hawk at first. Practice makes perfect!" (from Tibbets 1989, page 63) before laying the flat surface of the trowel up alongside the head of the first person who laughs." In the spirit of "ignorance is the father of invention", the senior author of this guide taught himself how to use a hawk without benefit of knowing how one was supposed to do it. And he unashamedly continues to use his "cheater" method to this day. It's simple. Standing on a ladder or scaffolding, and starting about 16 inches [40 cm] down from the top of the wall, press the further edge of the hawk against the wall. Using the trowel, cut away a slice of plaster from the further edge of the pile. Now, smear this material onto the wall with a graceful upward stroke of the trowel, continuing to press the edge of the hawk against the wall. Any plaster that doesn't stick to the bales will, miraculously, fall back onto the hawk for re-application. Resist the temptation to repeat the stroke with an "empty" trowel, as this will tend to weaken the bond of the wet plaster to the straw. However, you can repeat the "slice and smear" sequence, as necessary, to build up the desired thickness and to leave the reinforcement netting embedded in the plaster. Now, reposition the hawk to either side of your first stroke and repeat the process. As appropriate, drop down about 16 inches, or whatever you have now discovered is comfortable, and repeat the process. They may still laugh at your unprofessional style, but your shoes will probably be a lot cleaner than theirs will.

We were recently shown another novice-friendly technique by the lads at Bowerbird Construction, Dripping Springs, Texas. Their system avoids having to support the weight of several trowel-loads of plaster on the hawk, by dispensing with it. They use the side of a large pointed brick trowel to pick up and transfer plaster directly from the mortarboard,

or wheelbarrow, to the trowel. You know the rest.

Hand application is hard work, even for the pros, but "many hands can make lighter work". This is the time to call in your debts, to invite the participation of anyone who could conceivably be made to feel that they owed you a favor. Remind distant relatives of the importance of blood ties. Do whatever it takes to get a lot of help, at least with the scratch coat (the thickest of the three), or plan to be there a long time, painfully developing muscles that are good for little else.

Turning our focus now to **machine application**, we find a wide range of possibilities. The simplest is a hand-powered, hand-held, **"rough-casting" device** available, that we know of, in Mexico and in Europe. By turning a side-mounted handle, one splatters plaster onto the wall. The process leaves a rough surface that reputedly works well for a "scratch" coat. For more information, see *The Last Straw*, Issue 10, page 33, and Issue 11, page 34. Moving toward higher tech, there's the **hopper gun** used to blow texturing mixtures onto drywall. These consist of a pyramidal, plastic hopper to which is attached, at the bottom, a metal pistol grip and trigger, to which, in turn, is attached the hose from an air compressor. The plaster mix, which must be just thick enough so that the sand doesn't sink quickly to the bottom, is poured into the hopper. When the trigger is pulled, compressed air passes through the gun while at the same time an orifice is opened at the base of the hopper, allowing the soupy plaster to fall into the air stream and be blown out of the nozzle onto the wall. Before any pause of more than a couple of minutes, the hopper must be cleaned and the gun flushed out with water. Although this equipment produces good penetration, it takes a long time to get a significant layer built up. For maximum efficiency, there needs to be one person mixing, one pouring, and one spraying. This method is probably suited only for the scratch coat, where the excellent penetration is an obvious plus. A homemade, larger capacity version of the hopper gun technology is described in *The Last Straw,* Issue 13, page 14. A one-page set of detailed instructions can be obtained by sending a self-addressed, stamped envelope to *The Last Straw*, P.O. Box 42000, Tucson, AZ. 85733-2000.

Moving up to the semi-professional level, you could get yourself a **mini-pumper** such as the "Carrousel Pump", and the associated spraying equipment, made by Quikspray, Inc. of Port Clinton, Ohio, (419-732-2011). Although not capable of putting out as much volume as a full-size stucco pump, this system is safer, more easily portable, and much less expensive. We anticipate that regional straw-bale cooperatives or associations may soon be buying mini-pumpers for use by their members.

Which brings us to the "big toys for big boys", professional **stucco pump** level. They are big, expensive, dangerous to operate and can't be rented, but in the right hands can put a lot of plaster in place in a very short time. If you want good penetration, make sure that your plastering contractor has a rig that ejects the mix from the nozzle at high velocity. Not all pumps are created equal.

Finally, a few straw-bale buildings and privacy walls have been surfaced by professionals using a **"gunite pump"**, which mixes the dry materials (usually a fine-aggregate concrete mix) with water, right at the nozzle. The resulting material can be drier than that blown on with an ordinary stucco pump. This may make it possible to apply the base coat in a single layer, while still not getting an unacceptable amount of cracking.

As a part of "application", whether by hand or machine, decisions must be made about how to finish each successive layer. As the "scratch" coat begins to set up, horizontal scratches should be made in the surface to provide grooves for the "brown" coat to key into. As for the "brown" coat itself, the astute plasterer waits until the plaster has lost sufficient moisture so that the surface sheen has disappeared, but not so long that the plaster has become rigid. A type of trowel called a "float" is used to create a relatively even, open-textured surface. **Floating is considered by some to be the most important part of plastering**, since the consolidation that occurs during floating influences the shrinkage/cracking characteristics of the plaster.

Curing

Decisions must also be made about how quickly each of the first two coats should be followed by the next, and what should be done to ensure that each of the three coats "cures" properly to achieve maximum strength.

Modern practice dictates that the "brown" coat should be applied as soon as the "scratch" is sufficiently rigid to withstand the pressure needed to apply the "brown" without cracking. During this time, the "scratch" coat should be misted periodically to keep the surface damp. The spacing between mistings will be need to reflect the climate and the solar orientation of the wall. In extremely hot, dry, windy situations, it may be worth your trouble to cover the moistened, plaster surfaces with a plastic sheeting.

The "brown" coat should undergo moist curing for three days or more before the "finish" coat is applied to the moist, but still absorptive, surface. The moisture in the pre-dampened "brown" coat plus the water in the finish plaster itself will be enough to provide for the curing of this thin coat. To prevent variations in the color of this coat, do not apply any water to the finished surface until it has completely hardened.

An alternative to the sequence described above is called "scratch and back". Seattle's own straw-builder/architect, Ted Butchart, recommends this technique for owner-builders who want to use the "stucco party" ploy to get as much of the plastering done as possible in one day. Isn't it strange how few volunteers can be convinced to come back several days later to put on the "brown" coat? Didn't they have fun?

Anyway, the technique involves doing a slightly thinner than normal unscratched first coat. As soon as this has set up enough to withstand normal troweling (i.e., well before it has fully cured), you come back over it with the second coat. With enough mixing capability, tools and volunteers, the two-part base coast is in place at the end of the day.

Decorating

We will use this term to include various techniques one might use to go beyond the smooth, "mortician gray" appearance of the typical "brown" coat, or an unpigmented "finish" coat. We highly recommend that you stack and plaster a freestanding section of wall to use for experiments. Explore various options on this test "canvas" before decorating the real walls.

For the "brown" coat, the most commonly used techniques fall into the following categories:

• Staining—Although technically feasible, using **commercial concrete stains** to color an entire building might be prohibitively expensive. There are, however, several **less expensive alternatives** that have been tried (e.g., copper compounds, ferrous sulfate, ferric nitrate). Ferrous sulfate, used normally as a turf greener on golf courses, can often be purchased at stores selling fertilizers and agricultural chemicals. A saturated solution of ferrous sulfate, minus the yellow precipitate that accumulates on the bottom of the container, is applied to the wall with a brush or roller. It provides a range of colors from an orangy, mustard yellow to a reddish-brown, depending on the number of coats applied. It can also be used to stain concrete slabs. Another chemical, ferric nitrate, provides similar, but perhaps more vibrant colors. Unfortunately, being a strong oxidant, it can only be legally shipped as a hazardous chemical. This makes it harder to find and generally more expensive.

• Painting—Since it requires considerable hand-troweling skill to get a uniformly colored "finish" coat, some builders choose to roll or brush on a coat of **colored cementitious "paint"**. In Washington state, it's called a "fog coat" or "brush coat", and can be purchased, as a dry mix, from suppliers of masonry products. The aforementioned Ted Butchart sent us this simple recipe for a home-brewed version: mix 1 part cement (white cement for lighter tones), 1 part lime, and masonry pigments (or natural oxides), until uniform in color. Measure the ingredients very carefully to ensure color consistency between successive batches. Then add the dry mix to water until a brushable or rollable consistency is reached The plaster surface to which it is applied should be misted such that it is damp but still slightly absorptive. Using a saturated solution of ferrous sulfate as the liquid base of Ted's recipe might give nice results without additional pigments.

Also in the paint category, are **standard masonry paints** and the stretchy **elastomeric paints and coatings**. Depending on which one of these products is used, and how many coats are applied, you will lose some, or all, of the vapor permeability (breathability) that the plaster would otherwise have had. If you lose it all, no water, or water vapor, will be able to enter the plaster from the outside, an arguable plus. On the down side, no water, or water vapor, that finds its way into the plaster or the bale walls by whatever route, can escape to the outside through the paint layer. Most builders consider this a minus, and perhaps a serious one, especially in cold climates. Proceed with caution!

• Texturing/Sculpting—Textural modification of the "brown" coat itself is seldom seen in the U.S.A., except as an accent feature (e.g., around door and window openings). However, we have seen photos of a Nebraska Sandhills hay-bale house whose plaster was "tooled" to create the appearance of shaped, stone blocks. For accents, possibilities abound. For example, pulling a tool along to create grooves, pressing a "stamp" into the plaster to create repeated patterns., or sculpting to remove and/or add material.

• Accenting with Tiles—Although tiles can be incorporated into the "brown" coat, they are more commonly attached to the cured surface with special adhesives. The right angle formed by the edge of the tiles and the plaster surface is often filled in with some additional plaster, once the adhesive is fully set. If a "finish" coat is to be used, it can be thickened slightly around the tiles, leaving them flush with the final surface.

• Using a Colorant in the "Finish" Coat— This is the most common way to end up with colored walls when using cement-based plaster. Dry mixes can be purchased which already include the pigment(s), or these can be purchased separately and added during the mixing process. To avoid color variations between successive batches, great care must be taken not to vary the amounts of any of the ingredients, including the colorant.

• Modifying an Uncolored "Finish" Coat— Any of the methods described above for staining or painting the "brown" coat can also be used to modify an uncolored "finish" coat. Since this coat is relatively thin, white cement might be used instead of the more economical, gray Portland cement, in order to create a lighter-colored base for a stain or color wash.

Sealing

If rainfall will be repeatedly striking your walls, especially when propelled by high winds, you may want to consider sealing at least the lower portion of your walls with a product that will leave them water-repellent but still breathable. An obvious alternative, i.e.,covering the same part of the walls with a breathable housewrap, should serve the same purpose, but will prevent the plaster applied in those areas from keying into the roughness of the bale walls. Sealers intended for surface application are available from several manufacturers. Among them are Hill Brothers Chemical (Orange, CA, 714-998-8800), the Sinak Corporation (San Diego, CA, 619-231-1771), and El Rey Stucco Co. (505-873-1180).

Lime-Based Plasters

Recipes

Lime Putty Recipe

A lime putty is made by adding hydrated lime (type N or S) to an appropriate volume of water and leaving it undisturbed for at least 24 hours (the longer the better) while it develops "plasticity." Sifting the lime into the water through a window screen will break up any lumps in the dry material and prevent the formation of lumps that may form if the lime is simply dumped directly into the water. Before removing the putty for use in a plaster mix, it is convenient to remove most of the excess water, leaving enough, however, to always keep the top of the putty layer submerged. Steen et al (1994) suggest mixing five, 50 lb [22.7 kilos] bags of Type-N lime with water in a 55 gallon [208 liter] drum. If a good putty requires about seven gallons of water for each 50 lb bag of lime, as indicated by Van Den Branden and Hartsell (1984), you'll want about 35 gallons (160 liters) of water (i.e., a drum that is about two-thirds full).

Lime/Sand Mixes

Historically, lime-based plasters usually consisted of nothing but lime and sand. These plasters are slow to harden and slow to develop maximum strength. Typical mixes contained:

- one part lime putty,
- and, 3 to 4 parts clean plaster sand.

Lime/Sand Plaster with Cement as a Hardener

Because the traditional lime/sand plasters are slow to develop strength and hardness and often develop cracks, modern users often add a small percentage of Keene's cement (a type of gypsum) or Portland cement to provide greater initial strength and hardness. This approach was recently used on a two-story, timber-framed home in Vermont. Based on advice from the innovative folks at ARCHIBIO, in Quebec, the owner-builders (David Shaw and Juliet Cuming of Earth Sweet Home, W. Dumerston, VT) used this general recipe:

- 1 part of "lime/cement blend"
- 3 parts sand

In the first coat, which also contained chopped straw, the cement constituted 25% of the "blend", dropping to about 15% in the second coat and 5% in the final coat. They applied the plaster directly to the bales, using only burlap fabric as reinforcement around door and window openings.

Lime/Sand Plaster with Cactus Mucilage as a Stabilizer

The mucilagenous juice obtained by soaking the chopped up stems of cholla cactus or the chopped-up pads (nopales) of prickly pear cactus is traditionally used in Mexico to increase the durability of lime-based plasters. An article from DESIGNER/builder magazine (October 1994) describes how a master plasterer from Mexico, Pedro Sanchez, has used this plaster to protect historic adobe churches in New Mexico. He starts the process by soaking an unspecified amount of cholla stems for about six weeks in a covered, sun-warmed, 55-gallon [208 liter] drum filled with water. He then mixes together:

- 100 pounds [45.4 kilos] of lime (the article specifies type N),
- 50 shovels (probably round-nosed) of a coarse sand found locally in a dry streambed,
- and, 10 gallons [about 37.8 liters] of the gooey "cactus water".

The traditional three coats were then applied to the adobe walls, an approach that should also work directly over bales.

Mixing and Application

These plasters can be mixed either by hand or by machine. In Great Britain, they have traditionally been hand-mixed and then pounded with the end of a tool that resembles a baseball bat. The later process insures that all the sand grains become coated with wet lime. They are typically troweled on by hand, although use has been made of the previously mentioned, hand-powered, "rough-casting" device (see page 106).

As with cement-based plasters, the first coat should be scratched before it becomes too hard. When the "scratch" coat has set, the "brown" coat can be applied onto a slightly dampened surface. Unless compacted it will often crack as the putty shrinks. This is normally done a day after the coat has been applied, with a wooden float (trowel). Some oldtimers would drive a nail through the float, such that the point was barely exposed on the face, so that shallow scratches would be left to enhance the adhesion of the third coat.

The "finish" coat can be compacted either by troweling with a steel trowel, for a smoother finish, or by floating with a sponge float, for a grainy finish.

Curing

Since lime-based plasters cure and harden through contact with the atmosphere, they should be allowed to dry and set up between coats.

Decorating

Many of the techniques for decoration mentioned in the detailed discussion of cement-based plasters can be adapted for use with lime-based plasters, keeping in mind that the latter often have less cohesion. Only limeproof mineral pigments should be used as an admixture for the "finish" coat mix or to color a limewash. A colored limewash used over lime-based plaster by the above-mentioned Pedro Sanchez, consisted of 2 sacks of lime (presumably 50 lb [22.7 kg] bags of Type N) and a 1 lb [0.45 kg] bag of cement-and-mortar colorant. It was applied with a compressor-driven sprayer.

Gypsum-Based Plasters

(Non-)Recipes

Without set-retarding additives, gypsum hardens too quickly to allow for proper finishing. This makes it inconvenient and inefficient to create one's own gypsum plasters from "scratch", especially since time-tested, pre-mixed products are available. It can take considerable practice to acquire the skill needed to get the smooth, flawless surfaces that these products can produce. Start in places where your initial attempts will be least visible.

John Woodin, a respected straw-bale builder from Tucson, has developed a novice-friendly system for using a dual-purpose gypsum plaster for all three coats. The specific product he uses is called Double Duty Hardwall (James Hardy Co.). After installing expanded metal lath and stucco netting, as if for cement-based plaster, he applies a "scratch" coat mixed at a ratio of one bag of Double Duty, weighing 100 lbs [45.4 kilos] to 30 shovels of plaster sand. As soon as this sets, the same mix is used for the second coat. When this has fully cured, a final coat consisting of one bag of Double Duty plus one bag of 30-mesh silica sand, weighing 100 lbs [45.4 kilos], is troweled onto a slightly dampened surface. Pigment for coloring can be added to this coat. A brush is used to slightly moisten successive areas which are then brought to a smooth finish with a metal trowel.

A two-coat system for application onto adobe walls is described in Tibbets (1989, page 63). It calls for a fibered gypsum mix for the first coat, and an unfibered mix for the second one. For straw-bale walls, one might get good results by first doing an earthen plaster "scratch" coat. This would serve as a base for the two coats of gypsum applied, for example, as described in Servais (1986).

Mixing and Application

Again, mixing can be either by hand or machine, although certain types of finish mixes are traditionally mixed only on a mortarboard. On a residential scale, these plasters are usually applied by hand, although the first two coats are occasionally blown on.

Curing

Since the water that is needed to create a workable consistency is adequate to rehydrate the gypsum, these plasters do not require moist curing as do cement-based plasters. They must, however, be protected from drafts that dry the surface before rehydration is complete. If conditions are hot and windy, you may need to close all doors and windows, or tape cloth or plastic sheeting over their openings.

Decorating

Many of the techniques already described can also be adapted for use with gypsum-based plasters, taking into consideration their tendency to set comparatively rapidly. They are particularly suitable for raised relief sculpting and for treatment with "color washes". These usually consist of one part latex paint diluted with about 5 to 10 parts water. They can be applied in various ways (e.g., brush, mister, sponge, wadded cloth), singly or in combinations, and in one or more layers (see Innes 1992). Experiment on test panels until you get an effect you like, then start on your real walls.

Clay-Based Plasters

(Non-)Recipes

Soils can differ greatly in the amount and type of clay that they contain. For this reason, any specific recipe, whether from a book or from a friend, must be considered suspect, unless you will be using exactly the same materials as were used by the person that developed the recipe. For the same reason, we have chosen to risk your wrath by providing not formulas, but rather a brief guide for creating your own, by systematically experimenting with locally available materials.

Start experimenting early enough, so that you'll have the recipe worked out before the walls are ready to plaster. Your final soil mixture will probably end being about 65 to 80% sand and small pebbles, and 20 to 35% fine material (about half of which should be clay). As a general rule, too high a clay content will cause cracking as the plaster dries, while too little will result in an unacceptably weak final product. In practice, it is generally easier and less expensive to find and adjust a soil that has too much clay, than to "fix" one that has too little.

A quick method for estimating the clay content of a soil is described in Tibbets (1989, page 48). Another, the so-called "jar test", which gives an idea of the ratio of sand to silt to clay in a soil sample, is described on page 110 of the same source.

A more direct way to assess the plaster-potential of a soil is described below:

• Put your soil sample through a 1/4 inch [about 6 mm] screen to remove twigs, cigar butts, larger pebbles, etc. Mix about a quart [about 1 liter] of this screened soil sample with water.

• Adjust the ratio of soil to water to create a material that can be "smeared" on the side of a bale, with either your hand or a trowel. Create a patch about a foot square [30 by 30 cm], with a thickness of about a half inch [1.25 cm]. If the material won't stay on or doesn't have enough cohesion to maintain itself in a layer of this thickness, it has too little clay. You can chose to add various amounts of clay (either found or purchased) to this soil, but unless this is your last, best hope, eliminate this one and start again with a soil sample from a different location.

• If the material does meet the above requirements, allow the test patch to dry completely and then examine the results. Start by breaking off a chunk from one edge. If it breaks easily and the chunk crushes easily when squeezed between a thumb and forefinger, the clay content is too low. As above, consider eliminating it, at least temporarily.

• Let us assume that the patch offers adequate resistance to breaking and crushing (what degree of resistance is "adequate", only you can decide). Examine the surface for cracking. The spacing and depth of the cracks

will suggest how much sand (or sand and straw) must be added. If the cracking is minimal and shallow, try three test mixtures ranging from 1 part soil with 1/2 part sand, to 1 part soil with 1-1/2 parts sand. If the cracking is closely spaced and/or deep, try three mixtures bracketing 1 part soil with 4 parts sand. If the cracking is moderate, try three samples bracketing 1 part soil with 2-1/2 parts sand. You get the idea, eh?

Finding the "ideal" soil mixture often requires considerable trial and error, but it's worth the effort. When water is added to it, the result is a plaster that applies easily and sticks well to straw (has good adhesion) and to itself (has good cohesion). The final result will be a multi-layer coating that is strong, durable, and free from cracks.

Stabilizing

A bewildering array of compounds, both natural and synthetic, have been added to earthen plasters (with varying degrees of success) to reduce their erodability (i.e., increase their resistance to rain that hits and runs down the wall [see Tibbets 1989, pages 80-83]). The purpose of these "stabilizers" is to keep the surface from absorbing water and again becoming "mud", which is easily washed away. The characteristics of an ideal stabilizer would include that it be:

• inexpensive, if not free;
• non-toxic, easy and safe to use;
• low in embodied energy;
• made from something other than petroleum;
• able to "waterproof" the surface without diminishing its vapor permeability (a.k.a. breathability);
• water soluble initially, but insoluble after the plaster has dried.
• natural, rather than synthetic, and usable without extensive processing;

• free from negative effects on the color and appearance of the plaster;
  • resistant to solar radiation;
  • effective with a wide range of soil types;
  • and, regionally available, worldwide.

So there's the challenge. Come up with a stabilizer that meets even most of these criteria and the Nobel Prize for chemistry, or naturalchemy, is yours. In the meantime, the options aren't great. Until something better is found, the most commonly used stabilizer, at least in the overdeveloped world, will be emulsified asphalt (e.g., Chevron CSS-1). Be advised that the asphalt will darken the plaster slightly, chilling the warm earth tones a little. For many sand/soil mixes, the amount of emulsion needed falls in the range of from 3% to 5.5% of the weight of the dry mix. Going higher than 6% can significantly weaken the plaster. Knowing that these emulsions weigh about 8.3 pounds per gallon [1 kg per liter], will enable you to convert from weight required to volume required.

Adobe bricks are considered fully stabilized when they absorb no more than 2.5% of their initial dry weight when they sit on a water-saturated-surface for 7 days. A method for finding the minimum percentage of emulsion needed to achieve this degree of stabilization in bricks is described in Tibbets (1989, page 120). With minor adaptations, it can be used to test plaster samples as well.

A less rigorous approach involves adopting a procedure used successfully by someone else, in hopes that it will also work with your soil. You might try this one, adapted from pages 81 and 82 of the above-mentioned source:

• Use the trial-and-error process described earlier to develop a "proper" mix of clay-rich soil and sand.

• Determine, by experimentation, the amount of water needed to bring 7 shovels of the soil/sand mix to the proper consistency for plastering.

• Multiply this quantity of water by 10 to determine the correct amount for 70 shovels.

• To a plaster mixer (a real labor-saver that can often be rented), add 3/4 of the amount of water as determined immediately above, then add 2-1/2 gallons [9.5 liters] of emulsified asphalt.

• Now add 70 shovels of your mix, or the correct number of shovelfuls of sand and soil that maintain the proper ratio of sand to soil and that add up to 70.

• While continuing to mix, add water in small amounts until the desired consistency is reached.

• Test the "recipe" for erodability by spraying water on dry test patches using a garden hose and pistol-grip nozzle. Spray a patch of unstabilized plaster for comparison.

Clark Sanders of E. Meredith, NY, a veteran of three, owner-built, bale structures, has experimented with linseed oil as a stabilizer. His recipe involved 20 shovels of an earthen plaster mix, 5 gallons [about 19 liters] of chopped straw, 1 quart [about 1 liter] of boiled linseed oil, and water. Test panels were done with the recipe shown above, with this recipe minus the oil, and with this recipe minus both the oil and the straw. Testing indicates that both the oil and the straw help decrease the erodability of plaster and that the straw also helps to reduce cracking. He has concerns, however, about the degree to which the oil, in an amount sufficient to significantly reduce the erodability, will reduce the breathability.

Mixing and Application

Clay-based plasters can be mixed by hand or by machine. Although usually applied by hand (with either the hand or a trowel), they are occasionally "blown" on, using pumpers adapted especially for this purpose. Variations of this product have been referred to as Ablobe™ and Gun-Earth™. The hopper gun described on page 106 has also been used to blow on a soupy, earthen plaster mix to create a thin, well-integrated "scratch" coat.

In common practice, each coat is allowed to dry completely. This allows any cracking to take place before the surface is dampened and covered with the next coat. The dampening is critical to ensure a good "mud to mud" bond. Any dried coat which contains emulsified asphalt as a stabilizer will not absorb water (and turn to "mud"), so some users prefer to stabilize only the "finish" coat.

Curing

Since earthen plasters harden by drying out, they need no moist curing. However, to reduce cracking of a thick coat, time the application so that it will stay shaded from direct sunlight as long as possible and dry more slowly.

Decorating

• Painting—Standard, water- and oil-based paints do not adhere well to earthen plasters. To provide a paint-friendly surface on interior mud plaster, author Steve has brushed on a thick, creamy mixture of drywall joint compound (a gypsum-based material). It adheres well to earth plaster and interior latex paints are compatible with it. Limewashes (see page 111) have traditionally been used in Mexico as a "paint" for adobe brick and mud-plastered surfaces.

• Texturing/Sculpting—Because of the good cohesion of earthen plasters, and because their "set" can be delayed simply by keeping them moist, they are ideal for this type of decorating. The addition of chopped straw to the plaster will enable more heavily built-up areas and projections to stay attached to the wall. Some practioners have pushed slivers of bamboo into the wall, forming a kind of "armature" onto which the straw-heavy plaster is applied when considerable overhangs are wanted. Photo-illustrated books on international earth architecture (especially that from Africa) provide wonderful inspiration for the builders ready to turn their mud-plastered walls into a riot of color and texture (see Courtney-Clarke 1990).

• Rubbing Pigments onto a Light-Colored Finish Coat—The cover story of Issue 9 of *The Last Straw* describes a technique used by Santa Fe owner-builder Mark Cherry to create some of the most beautiful wall surfaces that author Matts has ever seen. In a nutshell, when his finish coat of buff-colored mud plaster had dried enough to be firm, but was still damp, he used the palm of his hand to rub natural mineral oxides (e.g., red iron oxide) into the drying plaster. Following this up later with a hand applied coat of a Livos brand oil, he sealed the entire surface and then developed a slight sheen in certain areas by applying a second coat of oil. The results are enviable!

• Using a Clay "Slip" on the Finish Coat—For the uninitiated, "slip" might connote a mistake or a piece of lingerie, but for Carole Crews and other aficionados of this technique, it means a creamy suspension of clay and other ingredients in water. Carole's home-based business in Taos, NM, specializes in the enhancement of mud-plastered walls through the use of sculpting and of slips that smooth, seal and brighten/lighten the walls.

For ingredients, her slips generally include:

• clay, either found locally or purchased from a supplier of pottery materials (e.g., white kaolin, especially good for making

light-colored slips);
- sand (always fine and generally light-colored);
- wheat paste, as a binder (homemade from flour [see below right], or purchased dry under the alias of wallpaper paste);
- and, fine particles of mica (KMG Minerals, Velarde, NM).

They may also include:
- a bit of chopped straw;
- larger flakes of mica;
- sodium silicate or powdered milk to keep the clay in suspension;
- pigments for coloration;
- and, in humid regions, borax in the wheat paste as a mold-preventer.

She mixes the ingredients in a large container, first filling it about 1/5 full with a thick, but pourable, water-based wheat paste. While stirring, water is then added until the pot is about 3/5 full. While continuing to stir, using a one-quart [one-liter] saucepan or coffee can as a scoop, she then adds about 3 scoops of clay, 1 scoop of fine sand and 1 to 2 scoops of mica. This process is repeated until the mixture has the consistency of "thick cream". If sodium silicate (or powdered milk) and/or straw are added at this point, a little additional water may also be required. At this point the ratio of ingredients may need to be adjusted somewhat. More sand can be added to give a rougher final surface (for a smooth surface, try omitting the sand).

The ideal surface on which to apply slips is one that is smooth and free from significant blemishes. Carole uses the following technique for creating such a surface. When the finish coat has been allowed to set up for just the right length of time (this is art, not science), she smooths out the mud plaster with a round-edged "tile sponge". After the finish coat is completely dry, the slip can then be applied.

Although traditionally applied with a piece of sheepskin, slips are now often painted on with a regular paint brush. Start at the top and work down. When the slip has partially dried, it too should be polished.

Take your tile sponge, dip it in water, wring it out and rub it lightly over the slip, using a circular motion to erase the brush marks. In order to not leave a film of clay over the straw and mica, she recommends rinsing and wringing out the sponge often. The results can be luminous!

Sealing

Sealers are used on **interior walls** primarily to keep the plaster from dusting. A clay slip containing wheat paste constitutes a non-dusting sealer. Wheat paste incorporated into the finish coat of earthen plaster will serve the same purpose. Cedar Rose of CRG Designs—Healthy Homes, in Carbondale, CO, makes her own wheat paste from organic, high gluten, unbleached, white flour. While the water in a big pot, two-thirds full, is coming to a boil, she adds to a gallon [3.8 liters] of cold water, a gallon of flour and two handfulls of vital gluten (available at natural food markets). While stirring, she then pours this mixture into the boiling water, continuing this process only until the blend becomes thick and transparent, at which time it can be added to mud plaster as it is being mixed. An expeditious, if not organic, alternative is dry wallpaper paste, mixed with water and used, just as is, as an additive during mixing.

Instead of incorporating the sealer into the plaster, one can also mist it on with a hand-held spray bottle, or maybe even a paint sprayer. This method has been used successfully with both wheat paste and with a half-and-half mixture of water and cheap white glue. Avoid too thick an application, unless you want the surface to have a sheen.

Sealers are used on **exterior walls** to water-proof the mud plaster or glue the surface particles together, thus preventing erosion. A waterproofing-type sealer recommended by its manufacturer for use on "earthen structures" is Crown 310 (El Rey Stucco Co. Albuquerque, NM). According to their literature, it "allows substrate to breathe". They also make a gluing-type sealer

called "Adobe Protector" that has been sprayed onto the mud plaster covering at least one straw-bale house. Several years after application, the user reported that it seemed to have been effective in preventing erosion, except where water was able to get into cracks and freeze. Since the effectiveness of any sealer may differ from one soil mixture to another, buy a small amount and test it on your plaster before making a big investment.

Photo by David Noble, Photographer, Santa Fe, NM

Step 8. Finishing Touches

Challenge: to create interior and exterior environments that are low-maintenance, low-cost, flexible, practical, healthy, comfortable, visually pleasing, personal and nurturing.

Walk-Through

• *At this point, with the building nearly finished and having learned from your mistakes, you might wish you could go back to Step 1. This time you would find an even simpler way to do it—a way that's customized to <u>you</u> as a builder/inhabiter. You would now have the advantage of knowing a fair amount about straw-bale construction, in addition to knowing much more about your unique situation than any "guide writer" ever could. Really, don't you wish we'd convinced you to start off with a little storage shed or a stand-alone guest bedroom, rather than a complete house? But, you've invested so much time, money, sweat and brain cells into getting to this point that, even though it's not perfect, you might as well finish it.*

♣ *Unless you chose to put interior partitions in before surfacing the interior walls, what you have now is an open space to be divided up according to your original floor plan (or some modification thereof). Consider doing the dividers (e.g., walls, screens) in such a way that they can be easily moved at some later time when your spatial needs and/or preferences have changed. Do any appropriate plumbing or electrical work before creating the finished surface on the partition walls.*

• *Most historic and modern bale builders have used thin frame walls, sheathed with*

gypsum plaster or sheet rock, to divide up their structures. They take up little of the interior floor space, and are cheap, quickly built, and easily moved or removed. If built with 2"X6"s [5X10 cm] they can comfortably accommodate gas and water pipes, drain pipes and plumbing vents. However, whether you use dimension lumber for partition walls or some of the other options listed on page 85, consider filling any voids in the walls with something that will increase their thermal mass and/or reduce the transmission of sound through them (e.g., sand, tamped straw, tamped straw coated with a clay slip).

• *If the natural color of the interior mud plaster is too dark for certain spaces, try a technique that author Steve and his wife, Nena, came up with for their straw-bale home. Mix powdered drywall joint compound with water to reach a consistency just thin enough to paint on with a wide, stiff brush. Be sure to get the mud plaster completely covered. When the joint compound is completely dry, roll or spray on an interior latex paint.*

♣ *Hang any wall-mounted cabinets, bookcases, etc.. If the wooden elements they will attach to are hidden under the plaster, use the map you made earlier (see page 83, upper left) to determine their location. Drill through the plaster to drive in dowels for the hanging of heavy artwork.*

As an alternative to hanging kitchen cabinets on irregular straw-bale walls, some builders have chosen to place against the bale wall a non-loadbearing, drywall-surfaced "veneer" wall. This provides vertical wooden studs from which the cabinets can be hung, and a smooth plane against which they can snugly fit. For more details on options for hanging and on alternatives to hanging, see the following two pages.

• Install any floor-standing cabinets, vanities, etc. As an alternative to the "veneer wall" strategy mentioned above, some builders prefer to put all floor-standing units in place after the "scratch" coat is applied, making sure to first patch any cracks in the area to be covered by the units. After you have protected the units with plastic sheeting, the second "brown" coat can then be used to fill any gaps between the back edge of the counter, or splash board, and the wall surface. An obvious disadvantage to this approach relates to future remodeling. If the wall area that has been hidden by the cabinets would then be exposed, considerable skill would be needed to then finish the plastering to match the rest of the wall.

• Install plumbing-related items and associated fixtures, louvered grilles over air ducts, vent fans, lights, ceiling fans, wood stoves for backup heating, cooling devices, etc. Continue with the seemingly interminable installation of shelves (for options see page 121), and hooks and rods for clothes, and the sanding, puttying, sanding, caulking, priming, sanding, painting, staining, et cetera.

• Don't ignore the outside. Get some herbs and a kitchen garden planted. Don't miss the right season to plant landscaping that will give you privacy, beauty, shade, and food (see EPA 1992, Moffat et al. 1995, and Groesbeck and Striefel 1997). Get your trees off to an early start. Add on any shade porches (see Making Your House a Home on page 122).

• Consider using bales to create other things you may want to complement your new home:
—a pump house, storage building, shop, studio space, guest house, sauna, etc.;
—a root cellar for extremely cold (and hot) regions;
—animal shelters;
—a solar oven or lumber kiln;
—a container for your compost pile;
—privacy walls (see Farrant 1996);
—and, outdoor seating.

• Accept the inevitable truth that Step 8 actually never ends—it just continues until you realize that what you are doing would be more honestly called "maintenance". Now you are either ready to avail yourself of the 12-step program that Straw-bale Builders Anonymous offers, or to continue with our 8-step program on a new and more elegantly-simple, straw-bale project. Don't be surprised to see one or both of us at the SBBA meetings or lurking around your job site hoping to pick up some tips for the next version of this guide. Bale well and prosper. And don't get too bent out of shape!

Hanging Things on Straw-Bale Walls

Duty Level	Pre-Plaster Planning?	Description of Option
light	not necessary	• for cement- or gypsum-based plaster, drill hole, insert nail; or drill hole, install plastic insert, attach something with a screw • for clay-based plaster, drill hole for dowel, pound in dowel, add screw on end for hanging; or once dowel in wall, attach something to it (e.g., telephone jack) phone jack dowel
medium	highly advisable advisable not necessary	• Gringo Grip™ (see page 87 for access info) May be O.K. for heavier loads, also. plaster stake • 2"X4" [5X10 cm] stake with flat side vertical or horizontal, depending on bale density plaster • drill hole, pound in dowel (not recommended for earth plaster) dowel
heavy	required	Shaker peg cut off end of stake, attach plywood "washer" kitchen cabinet attached to horizontal ledger boards plaster stucco netting attached to stake ledger board attached to wooden stake plaster
super-heavy	required	vertical 2"X4" [5X10 cm] "washer" in notch on outside surface 2"X4" [5X10 cm] ledgers in notch on inside surface, connected to "washer" with threaded rod

Alternatives to Hanging Things on Straw-Bale Walls

• Hang them from a normal partition wall or from a "veneer" wall (page 118, bottom right).

• Hang them from the roof/ceiling system.

• Have them rest on the floor (e.g., freestanding hutches, bookcases, backward bracket units [see below], storage units).

Special Options for Shelving on Straw-Bale Walls

• <u>Large-diameter (e.g., 1" [2.5 cm]) dowels driven into the bales.</u>

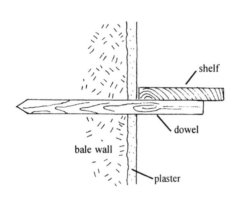

• <u>Metal track and bracket option:</u> normal mounting.

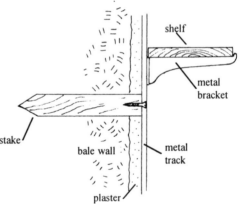

• <u>Metal track and bracket option:</u> backward bracket system.

1. Measure and cut vertical elements (2"X4" [5X10 cm]) for slightly loose fit.
2. Attach metal tracks.
3. Insert pin (e.g., nail with head removed) at top of one vertical element into small hole drilled at measured location in the drywall ceiling.
4. Move bottom end in toward wall until vertical.
5. Repeat steps 3 and 4 for all vertical elements.
6. Add brackets and shelves.

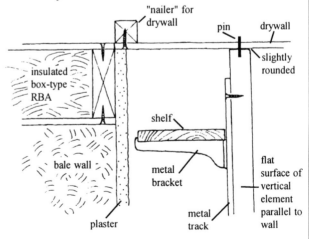

Making Your House a Home

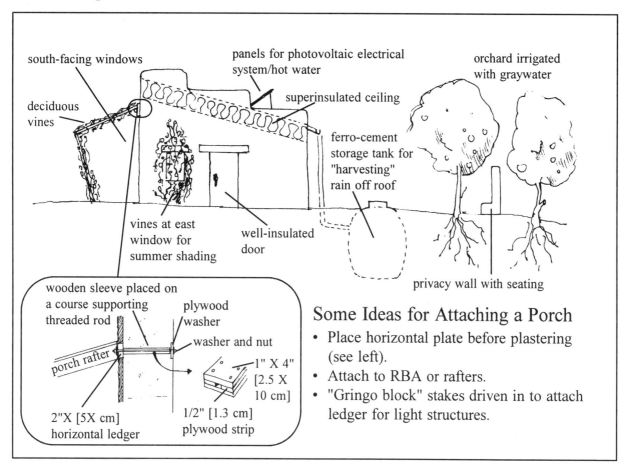

south-facing windows

panels for photovoltaic electrical system/hot water

orchard irrigated with graywater

deciduous vines

superinsulated ceiling

ferro-cement storage tank for "harvesting" rain off roof

vines at east window for summer shading

well-insulated door

privacy wall with seating

wooden sleeve placed on a course supporting threaded rod

plywood washer

washer and nut

porch rafter

1" X 4" [2.5 X 10 cm]

2"X [5X cm] horizontal ledger

1/2" [1.3 cm] plywood strip

Some Ideas for Attaching a Porch

- Place horizontal plate before plastering (see left).
- Attach to RBA or rafters.
- "Gringo block" stakes driven in to attach ledger for light structures.

Privacy Walls*

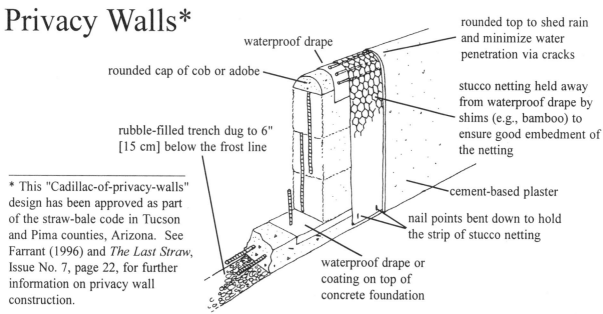

waterproof drape

rounded cap of cob or adobe

rounded top to shed rain and minimize water penetration via cracks

stucco netting held away from waterproof drape by shims (e.g., bamboo) to ensure good embedment of the netting

rubble-filled trench dug to 6" [15 cm] below the frost line

cement-based plaster

nail points bent down to hold the strip of stucco netting

waterproof drape or coating on top of concrete foundation

* This "Cadillac-of-privacy-walls" design has been approved as part of the straw-bale code in Tucson and Pima counties, Arizona. See Farrant (1996) and *The Last Straw*, Issue No. 7, page 22, for further information on privacy wall construction.

The Non-Loadbearing Option

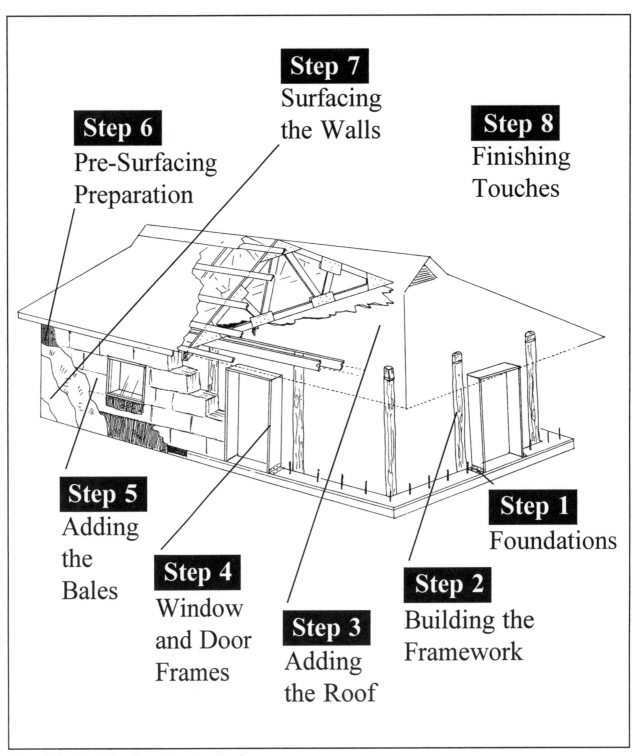

Step 7
Surfacing
the Walls

Step 6
Pre-Surfacing
Preparation

Step 8
Finishing
Touches

Step 5
Adding
the
Bales

Step 4
Window
and Door
Frames

Step 3
Adding
the Roof

Step 2
Building the
Framework

Step 1
Foundations

The Non-Loadbearing Option—An Introduction

In our description of the three basic approaches to straw-bale construction, we mentioned a number of possible advantages to the non-loadbearing approach. Here are several more reasons why some people have chosen this option:

• Their straw-bale code allows only this approach (e.g., New Mexico).

• They can't find an engineer who will put the required stamp on plans for a loadbearing design (e.g., seismically active California).

• The live loads (basically the snow loads) are so great that, even with a light roof/ceiling/insulation system, a safe span would be unacceptably short.

• The level of precision, plumbness, and straightness (e.g., of roof line or exposed rafter tails) demanded by the client or the builder would be impossible, difficult or unacceptably expensive (due to labor costs) to achieve with the loadbearing approach.

• They already owned a serviceable "old" structure to "outsulate" with "new" bales (see "temporal hybrids" on page 23).

Step 1. Foundations*

Challenge: to provide the same stable, durable base as in a loadbearing design. The details will differ, however, since the roof weight is now transmitted to the foundations by some kind of framework. If the framework involves widely spaced vertical posts, the foundations must be designed to handle the concentrated loads transferred at these points. The foundation must also properly elevate and carry the bale walls.

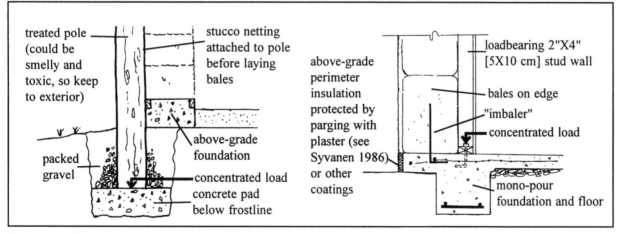

* As explained near the end of page 1, you really need to study the loadbearing approach first, to learn the generic techniques for working with bales. Having done that, return to this section for details unique to the non-loadbearing approach.

Step 2. Building the Framework

Challenge: to create a rigid, loadbearing framework to carry the roof weight and transfer it to the foundation. It should safely resist any horizontal (a.k.a. lateral) loads from wind or earthquakes. Multistory structures become easily possible.

In addition to occasionally carrying the total dead and live loads, the framework must also be able to resist lateral loads resulting from winds or earthquakes. With proper engineering, multistory structures become possible. The possibilities for frameworks run the gamut, from structural bamboo (a grass-like straw), to traditional wooden frames (studs, timbers, box posts, poles, etc.), to concrete block columns with a poured concrete bond beam, to steel posts topped with glue-laminated beams, to thin masonry walls or

panels. It is common practice that no additional tie-down system is used, provided the vertical elements of the framework are securely fastened to the foundation.

Most of these techniques are widely used and information on their "how to" is readily available. Recommended resources include Sherwood and Stroh (1992) and Wahlfeldt (1988) for wood frame; Benson (1990) for timber frame; NRAES (1984), Kern (1981), Wolfe (1993), and Sobon (1994) for post and pole.

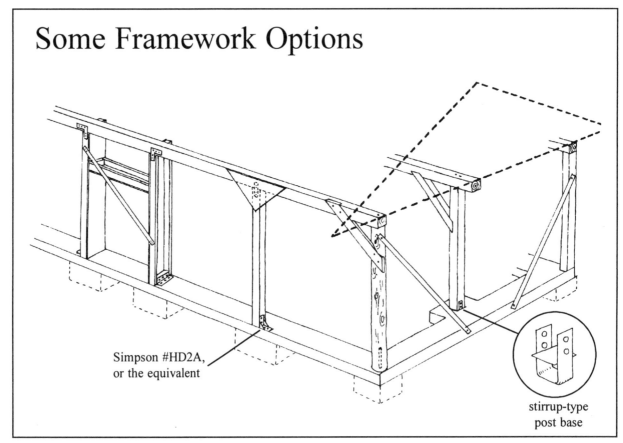

Some Framework Options

Simpson #HD2A,
or the equivalent

stirrup-type
post base

"After-The-Fact" Frameworks

The innovative lads and lassies at Daniel Smith and Associates, Berkeley, California, have been using an unusual method to create an inside-wrapped, diagonally-braced, 4"X4" [10X10 cm] post-and-beam framework, with the posts in notches. They reverse the normal sequence for the non-loadbearing approach, stacking the bales first, then cutting the notches, then installing the posts and the beams. This reversal enables them to raise the walls quickly and to mark and cut the notches in all the bales at the same time. Since the length of the posts can be finalized after the walls are up, the beam will always rest snugly against the tops of the walls—never a gap, or a space too narrow for the final course. For a sketch of a building utilizing their system, see *The Last Straw*, Issue No. 13, page 13.

Another version of this "framework after the fact" approach was used on a small studio in southern Arizona by Bob Cook and Friederike Almstedt. Around the perimeter of a plywood-on-shipping-pallet foundation/deck (see page 49) they attached three parallel lines of scrap 2"X4" [5X10 cm] pieces to form a toe-up. After stacking and pinning 3-tie bales, on edge, and installing a light, wooden RBA, they proceeded to weave 1"X2" [2.5X5 cm] furring strips (on 2' [61 cm] centers) down through the exposed ties. This was done on both sides of the wall. Along a given wall surface, the "over and under" sequence was reversed from one mini-column to the next. Once the furring strips were nailed securely to the RBA and to the sill plate, they not only supported any further dead and live load and tied the RBA to the foundation, but

also provided strips to which interior drywall and exterior sheathing could be attached. Despite their small cross-section, closely spaced, adequately constrained furring strips can carry a significant amount of load. For further details and photographs of this project, see Steen et al. (1994, page 76).

A technique that is similar, but which uses roughcut, full-dimension 1" X 4" strips to "sandwich" 2-tie bales laid flat, was developed by Bob Bissett in Bonner's Ferry, Idaho (see figure below). No pins were needed since the wood-and-wire "ladder trusses" provided adequate stiffening.

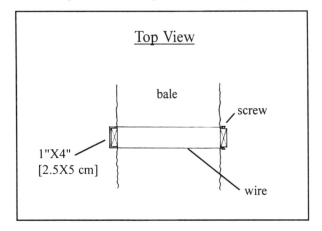

A short article about the construction of his storage shed, accompanied by excellent diagrams, appeared in *The Last Straw*, Issue No. 5, on page 14.

Drawing by Arlen Raikes

Options for Bale and Post Locations

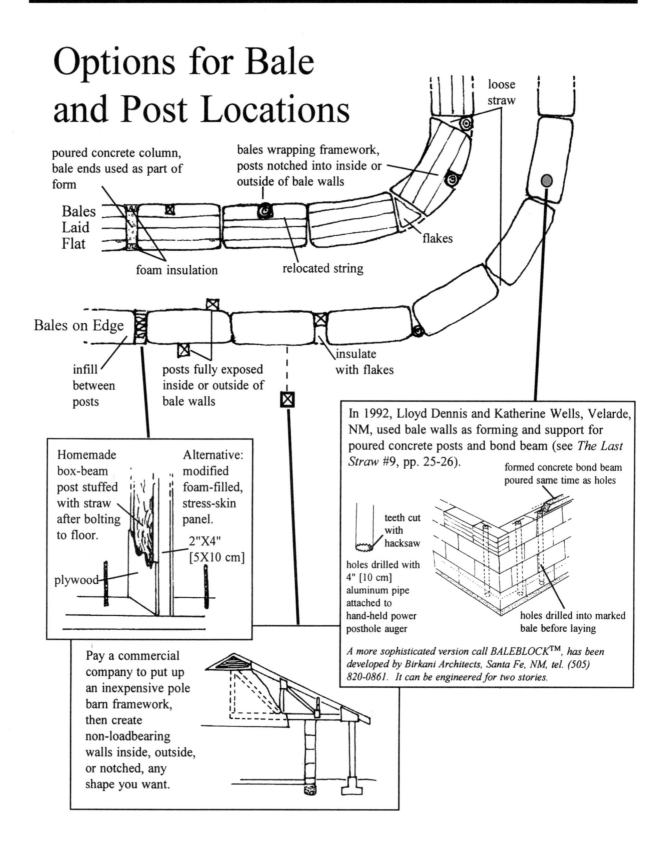

loose straw

poured concrete column, bale ends used as part of form

bales wrapping framework, posts notched into inside or outside of bale walls

Bales Laid Flat

foam insulation

relocated string

flakes

Bales on Edge

infill between posts

posts fully exposed inside or outside of bale walls

insulate with flakes

Homemade box-beam post stuffed with straw after bolting to floor.

plywood

Alternative: modified foam-filled, stress-skin panel.

2"X4" [5X10 cm]

Pay a commercial company to put up an inexpensive pole barn framework, then create non-loadbearing walls inside, outside, or notched, any shape you want.

In 1992, Lloyd Dennis and Katherine Wells, Velarde, NM, used bale walls as forming and support for poured concrete posts and bond beam (see *The Last Straw #9*, pp. 25-26).

teeth cut with hacksaw

holes drilled with 4" [10 cm] aluminum pipe attached to hand-held power posthole auger

formed concrete bond beam poured same time as holes

holes drilled into marked bale before laying

A more sophisticated version call BALEBLOCK™, has been developed by Birkani Architects, Santa Fe, NM, tel. (505) 820-0861. It can be engineered for two stories.

Step 3. Adding the Roof

Challenge: to create the same sheltering cap as in the loadbearing option, although using a non-compressible framework does release you from some of the constraints inherent in loadbearing designs (e.g., total roof weight).

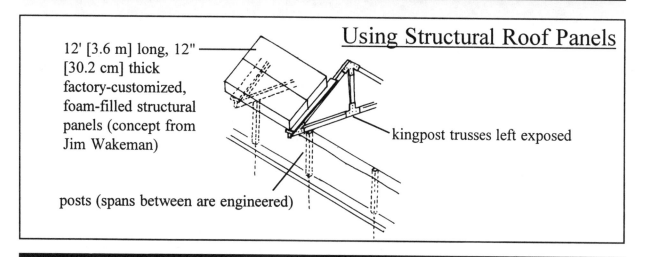

Using Structural Roof Panels

12' [3.6 m] long, 12" [30.2 cm] thick factory-customized, foam-filled structural panels (concept from Jim Wakeman)

kingpost trusses left exposed

posts (spans between are engineered)

Step 4. Window and Door Frames

Challenge: to create suitable door and window frames for all openings. Since no portion of the roof load is carried by the frames, and since all the needed wall rigidity can be built into the framework, there is freedom to make the openings larger and/or more numerous. The perceived desirability of this must be balanced against the relatively low R-value of doors and windows (even in the most expensive, high-tech models), and the resulting negative effect on the performance of your superinsulated building.

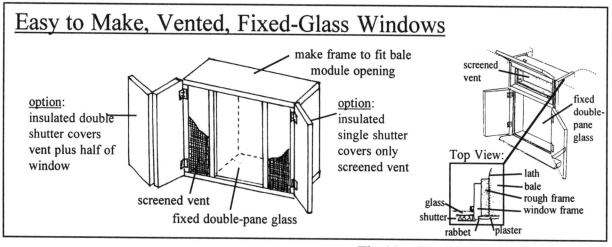

Easy to Make, Vented, Fixed-Glass Windows

make frame to fit bale module opening

option: insulated double shutter covers vent plus half of window

option: insulated single shutter covers only screened vent

screened vent

fixed double-pane glass

screened vent

fixed double-pane glass

Top View:

lath
bale
rough frame
window frame

glass
shutter
rabbet
plaster

Step 5. Adding the Bales

Challenge: to create walls that are properly stacked, pinned (often with shorter pins), and attached to the framework. Having posts or columns makes it easier to create vertical walls, but there's extra work in attaching the walls to the framework. For certain placements of posts, the bales must be notched to receive them.

Bales Flat versus On-Edge

Bale Flat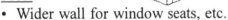

Pros:
- Wider wall for window seats, etc.
- More stable (especially for 2-tie bales).

Cons:
- Takes up more space.
- Takes more bales.

Bale On-Edge

Pros:
- Takes fewer bales.
- Less space lost to wall.

Cons:
- More susceptible to fire or vandalism before covered.

Tools for Cutting Notches

bow saw

machete

chainsaw (*Tip*: if electric, cutting with top of blade prevents plugup problems)

relocate the top string to permit notching for large posts

Four-inch grinder with cable-twist wire wheel or Lancelot cutter blade

hay knife

Attaching a Bale Wrap to the Framework

Many approaches have been used. Be creative.

Top View

Side View

rebar stub or stucco netting wired to stud of standard frame

bales wired to eye bolt or equivalent
(technique especially helpful at corners)

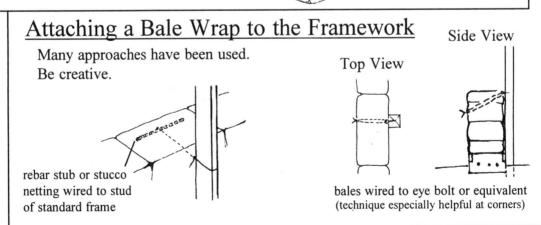

Attaching an Infill Panel to the Posts

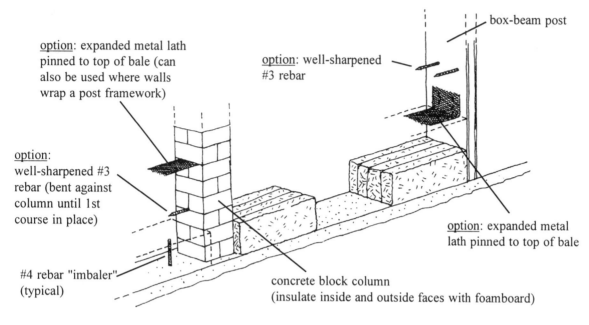

option: expanded metal lath pinned to top of bale (can also be used where walls wrap a post framework)

option: well-sharpened #3 rebar

box-beam post

option: well-sharpened #3 rebar (bent against column until 1st course in place)

option: expanded metal lath pinned to top of bale

#4 rebar "imbaler" (typical)

concrete block column (insulate inside and outside faces with foamboard)

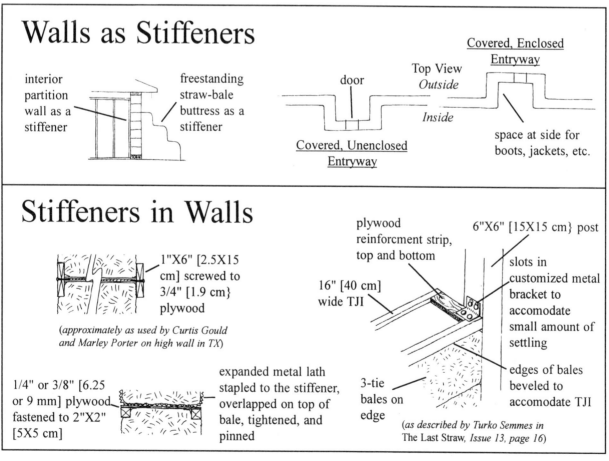

Walls as Stiffeners

interior partition wall as a stiffener

freestanding straw-bale buttress as a stiffener

door

Top View
Outside

Covered, Enclosed Entryway

Inside

Covered, Unenclosed Entryway

space at side for boots, jackets, etc.

Stiffeners in Walls

1"X6" [2.5X15 cm] screwed to 3/4" [1.9 cm} plywood

(approximately as used by Curtis Gould and Marley Porter on high wall in TX)

1/4" or 3/8" [6.25 or 9 mm] plywood fastened to 2"X2" [5X5 cm]

expanded metal lath stapled to the stiffener, overlapped on top of bale, tightened, and pinned

plywood reinforcment strip, top and bottom

16" [40 cm] wide TJI

3-tie bales on edge

6"X6" [15X15 cm} post

slots in customized metal bracket to accomodate small amount of settling

edges of bales beveled to accomodate TJI

(as described by Turko Semmes in The Last Straw, Issue 13, page 16)

Step 6. Pre-Surfacing Preparation

Challenge: to accomplish all tasks that need to precede surfacing the walls, as dictated by the surfacing material chosen, decisions about use of moisture barriers and reinforcement, etc.

If you choose to plaster your walls, the techniques are the same as described in *The Loadbearing Option, Step 7*, except that in some cases you will have the vertical elements of the framework to attach netting to. If you choose to cover your walls with drywall (Do you really want your walls looking that sterile?), paneling, siding, or board-and-batten, you will need furring strips (or the equivalent) attached to the walls. See the diagram to the right for possibilities.

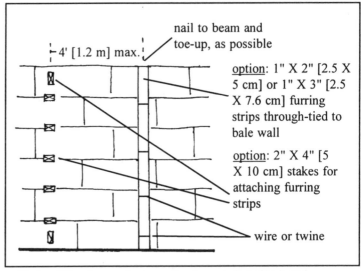

nail to beam and toe-up, as possible

├─ 4' [1.2 m] max. ┤

option: 1" X 2" [2.5 X 5 cm] or 1" X 3" [2.5 X 7.6 cm] furring strips through-tied to bale wall

option: 2" X 4" [5 X 10 cm] stakes for attaching furring strips

wire or twine

(for two different approaches to creating the equivalent of horizontal furring strips, see *The Last Straw*, Issue 6, page 21, and Issue 7, page 24)

Step 7. Surfacing the Bales

Challenge: as in a loadbearing design, to protect the wall surfaces from the elements, the occupants, infestation by vermin, and depredation by vandals or livestock.

Step 8. Finishing Touches

Challenge: to get your home finished, while resisting the temptation to move in until the interior is really completed. Once you're moved in, life has a way of providing what seem to be higher priorities than getting that mortician-gray concrete floor stained and waxed, or caulking and painting in the bedroom (nobody but you sees it anyway, right?).

Literature Cited

ACHP. 1995. Northern comfort: advanced cold climate home building techniques. Alaska Craftsman Home Program, Inc., Anchorage, AK. 288 p.

Alexander, C. 1977. A pattern language. Oxford University Press, New York, NY. 1171 p.

_____. 1979. The timeless way of building. Oxford University Press, New York, NY. 352 p.

Alfano, S. 1985. The art and science of estimating. Fine Homebuilding, 6/85:32-35.

Anderson, B., and **M. Riordan.** 1996. The new solar home book. Brick House Publ. Co., Amherst, NH. 204 p.

ARCHIBIO. 1995a. The ecotoilet. ARCHIBIO, 6282 St. Vallier, Montreal, Quebec, Canada, H2S 2P5. 7 p. pamphlet.

_____. 1995b. A home-grown roof: the hair on your house. The Last Straw 12:33-34.

_____. 1995c. The living roof. ARCHIBIO, see above for access.

_____. 1995d. The strawbale slab. ARCHIBIO, see above for access.

Bee, B. 1997. The cob builder's handbook. Publisher: Becky Bee, Box 381, Murphy, OR, 97533. About 100 p.

Benson, T. 1990. The timber-frame home: design, construction and finishing. The Taunton Press, Newtown, CT. 240 p.

Berglund, M. 1985. Soil-cement tile floor. Fine Homebuilding 6/85:56-59.

Black, E. 1996. Empowering the borrower. Abundance Press, Flagstaff, AZ (tel. 520-526-2432). 102 p.

Bolles, B. 1996. The straw-bale workbook: a guide to building a house of straw bales. Bale Press, Poway, CA. 232 p. (tel. 619-486-6949.)

Bower, J. 1993. Healthy house building: a design and construction guide. The Healthy House Institute, Bloomington, IN. 384 p.

_____. 1995. Understanding ventilation: how to design, select and install residential systems. Healthy House Institute, Bloomington, IN. 432 p.

Brown, A. 1993. Small spaces: stylish ideas for making more of less in the home. Kodansha America, New York, NY. 96 p.

Burns, M. 1993. Cottage water systems: an out-of-the-city guide to pumps, plumbing, water purification and privies. Firefly Books, Ltd., Buffalo, NY. 160 p.

Carmody, J., S. Selkowitz, and **L. Heschong.** 1996. Residential windows. Norton and Co., New York, NY. 214 p.

Cauldwell, R. 1996. Wiring a house. The Taunton Press, Newtown, CT. 248 p.

Cecchettini, P. J. Wood, and **B. Beckstrom.** 1989. Home plans for solar living. Home Planners, Inc., Farmington Hills, MI. 192 p.

Clegg, P., and **D. Watkins.** 1987. Sunspaces. Storey Communications, Pownal, VT. 206 p.

CMHC. 1994. Moisture in Atlantic housing. Canadian Mortgage and Housing Corporation, Ottawa, Ontario, Canada. 146 p.

_____. 1995. Building materials for the environmentally hypersensitive. Canadian Mortage and Housing Corporation, Ottawa, Ontario, Canada. 238 p.

Cole, J., and **C. Wing.** 1976. From the ground up. Little, Brown and Co., Boston, MA. 244 p.

Connell, J. 1993. Homing instinct: using your lifestyle to design and build your home. Warner Books, New York, NY. 404 p.

Cook, J. 1989. Passive cooling. MIT Press, Cambridge, MA. 593 p.

Courtney-Clarke, M. 1990. African canvas: the art of West African women. Rizzoli, New York, NY. 204 p.

Crocker, E. 1995. Straw daubs: how fiber cuts erosion in mud plasters. The Last Straw 9:11.

Curran, J. 1979. Drawing plans for your own home. Brooks Publ. Co., Bakersfield, CA. 227 p.

Day, C. 1990. Places of the soul: architecture and environmental design as a healing art. Aquarian Press, Wellingborough, England. 192 p.

Dickinson, D. 1996. Small houses for the next century. McGraw Hill, New York, NY. 244 p.

Easton, D. 1996. The rammed earth house. Chelsea Green Publishing Co., White River Junction, VT. 272 p.

Eisenberg, D. 1995. Straw-bale construction and the building codes: a working paper. Development Center for Appropriate Technology, Tucson, AZ. 30 p.

EPA. 1992. Cooling our communities: a guidebook on tree planting and light-colored surfacing. Environmental Protection Agency, Superintendent of Documents, P.O. Box 371954, Pittsburgh, PA, 15220-7954.

Erickson, J. 1989. The homeowner's guide to drainage control and retaining walls. Tab Books, Blue Ridge Summit, PA. 152 p.

Farrant, T. 1996. How to build straw bale landscape and privacy walls. Self-published. Access: OOB-By Mail, 1039 E. Linden St., Tucson, AZ, 85719. 21 p. booklet.

Feirer, M. 1986. Making a structural model. Pages 2-5, *in* Construction techniques 2. The Taunton Press, Newtown, CT. 232 p.

Ferguson, M. 1996. Drywall: professional techniques for walls and ceilings. Taunton Press, Newtown, CT. 144 p.

Gibson, S. 1994. Air and vapor barriers. Fine Homebuilding, 4/94:48-53.

Givoni, B. 1994. Passive and low-energy cooling of buildings. Van Nostrand Reinhold, New York, NY. 264 p.

Good Wood Alliance. 1996. Good wood directory. Good Wood Alliance, Burlington, VT, 05401. 32p. (802) 862-4448 or warp@together.net).

Greenlaw, B. 1994. Sizing up housewraps. Fine Homebuilding 11/94:42-47.

Groesbeck, W., and **J. Striefel.** 1997. The resource guide to sustainable landscapes and gardens. Environmental Resources, Inc.. Salt Lake City, UT. 486 p.

Gross, M. 1989. Roof framing. Craftsman Book Co., Carlsbad, CA 475 p.

Hageman, J. 1994. Contractor's guide to the building code. Craftsman Book Co., Carlsbad, CA. 544 p.

Hamilton, G., and **K. Hamilton.** 1991. How to be your own contractor. MacMillan, Old Tappan, NJ. 192 p.

Harland, E. 1994. Eco-renovation: the ecological home improvement guide. Chelsea Green Publishing Co., White River Junction, VT. 288 p.

Harris, B. J. Ongoing. The Harris directory: recycled content building materials. Disk for PC's. 508 Jose St., #913, Santa Fe, NM, 87501-1855.

Heldman, C. 1996. Be your own house contractor. Third Edition. Storey Publishing Co., Pownal, VT. 144 p.

Herbert, R. D. 1989. Roofing: design criteria, options, selection. R. S. Means, Kingston, MA. 223 p.

Houlen, H., and **H. Guillard.** 1994. Earth construction: a comprehensive guide. IT Publications, London. 362 p.

Householder, J., and **J. Moulton.** 1992. Estimating for home builders. Craftsman Book Co., Carlsbad, CA. 181 p..

HUD (US Dept. of Housing and Urban Development). 1995. Design guide for frost-protected shallow foundations. Available from HUD-User, P. O. Box 6091, Rockville, MD 20849 as Order #ACCN-HUD6512.. (Call toll-free at 1-800-245-2691, or download from either <http://www.cs.arizona.edu/people/jcropper/desguide.html>, or <gopher://huduser.aspensys.com73>).

Innes, J. 1992. The new paint magic. Pantheon Books, New York, NY. 239 p.

Jackson, M. 1990. The good house: contrast as a design tool. The Taunton Press, Newtown, CT. 147 p.

Jackson, W. P. 1979. Building Layout.

Craftsman Book Co., Carlsbad, CA. 238 p.

Jenkins, J. 1994. The humanure handbook. Jenkins Publishing, Grove City, PA. 198 p.

Kennedy, J. 1996. Earth shoes. The Last Straw 16:10.

Kern, K. 1975. The owner built home. Charles Scribner's Sons, New York, NY. 374 p.

Kilpatrick, J. 1989. Understanding house construction. Home Builder Press of NAHB, Washington, D.C. 79 p.

King, B. 1996. Buildings of earth and straw: structural design for rammed earth and straw-bale architecture. Ecological Design Press, Sausalito, CA. Distributed by Chelsea Green Publishing Co., White River Junction, VT. 169 p.

Klippenstein, A., and **P. Lacinski**. 1996. Regional identity: questions for the Nebraska-style house. The Last Straw 13:6-8.

Kolle, J. 1995. Choosing roofing. Fine Homebuilding 1/95:46-51.

Lanning, B. 1995. Straw bale portfolio: a collection of sixteen designs for straw-bale houses. Self-published. Available from Out On Bale-By Mail, 1037 E. Linden St., Tucson, AZ 85719.

Laporte, R. 1993. Mooseprints: a holistic home building guide. The Natural Home Building Center, Santa Fe, NM. 35 p.

Law, T. 1982. Site layout. Fine Homebuilding 10/82:26-28.

Lechner, N. 1991. Heating, cooling, lighting: design methods for architects. John Wiley & Sons, New York, NY. 524 p.

Lenchek, T., C. Mattock, and **J. Raabe.** 1987. Superinsulated design and construction: a guide for building energy-efficient homes. Van Nostrand Reinhold, New York, NY. 172 p.

Lerner, K. 1997. Banking on a vault. The Last Straw 17:9+.

Levin, A. H. 1991. Hillside building: design and construction. Arts & Architecture Press, Santa Monica, CA. 172 p.

Loomis, H. 1991. Single-ply roofing. Fine Homebuilding 1/91:43-47.

Loy, T. 1983. Understanding concrete. Fine Homebuilding 2/83:28-32.

Lstiburek, J. 1997. Energy efficient building guide: cold climates. Energy Efficient Building Association, Minneapolis, MN. 276 p.

Lstiburek, J., and **J. Carmody.** 1993. Moisture control handbook: principles and practices for residential and small commercial buildings. Van Nostrand Reinhold, New York, NY. 214 p.

Ludwig, A. 1994. Create an oasis with greywater: your complete guide to managing greywater in the landscape. Second Expanded and Revised Edition. Oasis Design, 5 San Marcos Trout Club, Santa Barbara, CA, 93105-9726. 49 p.

Luttrell, M. 1985. Warm floors. Fine Homebuilding 6/85:68-71.

Lynch, K., and **G. Hack.** 1984. Site planning. MIT Press, Cambridge, MA. 499 p.

Malin, N. 1995a. Building lightly on the land. The Last Straw 11:9.

_____. 1995b. Frost-protected shallow foundations. Environmental Building News 4(4):10-11.

_____. 1995c. Roofing materials: a look at the options for pitched roofs. Environmental Building News 4(4):1+.

Marinelli, J., and **P. Bierman-Lytle.** 1995. Your natural home: a complete sourcebook and design manual for creating a healthy, beautiful, and environmentally sensitive house. Little Brown and Co., New York, NY. 272 p.

Marshall, B., and **R. Ague.** 1981. The super-insulated retrofit book: a home-owners guide to energy-efficient renovation. Firefly Books, Willowdale, Ontario, Canada. 208 p.

Massey, H. 1994. Basic plumbing. Craftsman Book Co., Carlsbad, CA. 384 p.

McHarg, I. L. 1995. Design with nature. John Wiley & Sons, New York, NY. 208 p.

McHenry, P. G. 1985. Adobe: build it yourself. Univ. of Arizona Press, Tucson, AZ. 158 p.

_____. 1989. Adobe and rammed earth buildings: design and construction. Univ. Arizona Press, Tucson, AZ. 217 p.

Melander, J., and **A. Isberner.** 1996. Portland

cement (stucco) manual. Portland Cement Association, Skokie, IL. 50 p.

Metz, D. 1991. New compact house designs. Storey Com., Inc., Pownal, VT. 192 p.

Moffat, A., M. Schiler, and the **staff of Green Living.** 1995. Energy-efficient and environmental landscaping. Appropriate Solutions Press, South Newfane, VT. 240 p.

Mollison, B. C., and **R. M. Slay.** 1988. Permaculture: a designers' manual. Tagari, Tyalgum, Australia.

Monahan, E. J. 1986. Construction of and on compacted fills. John Wiley & Sons, New York, NY. 200 p.

Mumma, T. 1997. Guide to resource efficient building materials. Center for Resourceful Building Technology, Missoula, MT. 120 p.

MWPS (Midwest Plan Service). 1989a. Designs for glued trusses. Midwest Plan Service, Ames, IA. 84 p.

_____. 1989b. Farm and home concrete handbook. MWPS-35. Iowa State University, Ames, IA. 46 p.

Nisson, J. D. N. 1990. Radiant barriers. Cutter Information Corp., Arlington, MA. 140 p.

Nisson, J. D. N., and **G. Dutt.** 1985. The superinsulated home book. John Wiley & Sons, New York, NY. 306 p.

NRAES (Northeast Regional Agricultural Engineering Service). 1984. Pole and post buildings: design and construction handbook. NRAES-1. Available through Midwest Plan Service, Iowa State University, Ames, IA. 47 p.

Pacey, A., and **A. Cullis.** 1986. Rainwater harvesting: the collection of rainfall and run-off in rural areas. Intermediate Technology Publ., London, England. 216 p.

Pearson, D. 1989. The natural house book: creating a healthy, harmonius and ecologically sound home environment. Simon and Schuster, New York, NY. 287 p.

_____. 1996. The natural house catalog. Fireside Books, New York, NY. 287 p.

Pinsky, M. 1995. The EMF book: what you should know about electromagnetic fields,

electromagnetic radiation and your health. Warner Books, New York, NY. 256 p.

Potts, M. 1993. The independent home: living well with power from the sun, wind and water. Chelsea Green Publ. Co., Post Mills, VT. 300 p.

Reed, S., C. Crites, and **E. J. Middlebrooks.** 1994. Natural systems for waste water management and treatment. McGraw-Hill, New York, NY.

Reynolds, M. 1990. Earthship, volume I: how to build your own. Solar Survival Press. Taos, NM. 229 p.

_____. 1991. Earthship, volume II: systems and components. Solar Survival Press, Taos, NM. 255 p.

Ring, D. 1990. Brick [on sand] floors. Pp. 94-97, *in* Foundations and masonry (J. Lively, ed.). The Taunton Press, Newtown, CT. 127 p.

Roskind, R. 1983. Before you build. Ten Speed Press, Berkeley, CA. 240 p.

Roy, R. 1992. Cordwood masonry housebuilding. Sterling Publishing Co., New York, NY. 255 p.

Ruez, J. 1995. Preparations for stuccoing a straw-bale building. The Last Straw 9:9-10.

Sanders, S. 1993. Staying put: making a home in a restless world. Beacon Press, Boston, MA. 203 p.

SBCA (Straw Bale Construction Association). 1994. The New Mexico engineering tests, thermal conductivity testing and draft building code. Straw Bale Construction Association, Santa Fe, NM. Various pagings. (Also available from OOB-By Mail, Tucson, AZ. tel. 520-624-1673.)

Servais, J. 1986. Two-coat plaster. Fine Homebuilding 3:58-62.

Shephard, J. 1992. Be your own contractor. Dearborn Trade, Chicago, IL. 315 p.

Sherwood, E., and **R. Stroh.** 1992. Wood frame house construction: a do-it-yourself guide. Sterling Publishing Co., New York, NY. 306 p.

Siegenthaler, J. 1995. Modern hydronic heating. Delmar Publishers, Albany, NY. 448 p.

Smith, M. 1997. The cobber's companion. Cob

Cottage Company, Box 123, Cottage Grove, OR, 97424. 100 p.

Smith, N. 1995. Small space living design. Rockport Publications, Rockport, MA. 128 p.

Smulski, S. 1994. All about roof trusses. Fine Homebuilding 6/94:40-45.

Sobon, J. 1994. Build a classic timber-framed house. Storey Comm., Inc., Pownal, VT. 208 p.

Spence, W. P. 1993. Architectural working drawings: residential and commercial buildings. John Wiley & Sons, New York, NY. 521 p.

Steen, A., and **B. Steen.** 1997a. Earthen and lime plasters. The Canelo Project, HC 1, Box 324, Elgin, AZ, 85611. (Tel. 520-455-5548; Fax 520-455-9360; E-mail absteen@dakotacom.net). Unpaginated booklet.

_____. 1997b. Earthen floors. The Canelo Project (for access see Steen and Steen, 1997a). Unpaginated booklet.

_____. 1997c. Natural paints and wall finishes. The Canelo Project (for access see Steen and Steen, 1997a). Unpaginated booklet.

Steen, A. S., B. Steen, D. Bainbridge, with **D. Eisenberg.** 1994. The straw bale house. Chelsea Green Publ. Co., White River Junction, VT. 297 p.

Strang, G. 1983. Straw bale studio. Fine Homebuilding 12/83:70-72.

Strong, S. 1994. The solar electric house book: a design manual for home-scale photovoltaic power systems. Sustainability Press, Still River, MA. 288 p.

Stulz, R., and **K. Mukerji.** 1993. Appropriate building materials. Third Edition. SKAT/Intermediate Technology Publications, St. Gallen, Switzerland/London, UK and Women Ink, New York, NY. 430 p.

Syvanen. 1983. Small-job concrete. Fine Homebuilding 2/83:34-35.

_____. 1986. Insulating and parging foundations. Pp. 179-181, _in_ Construction techniques 2. The Taunton Press, Newtown, CT. 232 p.

160 p.

Thoreau H. D. 1950. Walden-civil disobedience. Rinehart & Co., New York, NY. 304 p.

Tibbets, J. 1989. The earthbuilders' encyclopedia. Southwest Solaradobe School, Bosque, NM. 196 p.

Tom, R. 1996. Rocks in your shoes. The Last Straw 16:7.

Traister, J. 1994. Residential electrical design-revised. Craftsman Book Co., Carlsbad, CA. 256 p..

Van Den Branden, F., and **T. Hartsell.** 1984. Plastering skills. American Technical Publishers, Homewood, IL. 543 p.

Van der Ryn, S. 1995. The toilet papers: recycling waste and conserving water. Ecological Design Press, Sausalito, CA. 128 p.

Velonis, E. 1983. Rubble-trench foundations. Fine Homebuilding 12/83:29-31.

Venolia, C. 1995. Healing environments: your guide to indoor well-being. Celestial Arts, Berkeley, CA. 240 p.

Wahlfeldt, B. 1988. Wood frame house building: an illustrated guide. Tab Books, Blue Ridge Summit, PA. 262 p.

Walters, D. 1991. Feng shui handbook: a practical guide to Chinese geomancy. Aquarian Press, UK. Thorsons, San Francisco, CA. 224 p.

Weidhass, E. R. 1989. Architectural drafting and construction. Allyn and Bacon, Boston, MA. 575 p.

Welsch, R. L. 1970. Sandhill baled-hay construction. Keystone Folklore Quarterly, Spring Issue, 1970:16-34.

_____. 1973. Baled Hay. Page 70, _in_ Shelter (L. Kahn, ed.). Shelter Publications, Bolinas, CA. 176 p.

Whitten, B. 1991. How to hire and supervise subcontractors. Second edition. Home Builder Press, Washington, D.C. 60 p.

Wilson, A. 1995a. Insulation materials: environmental comparisons. Environmental Building News 4(1):1+.

_____. 1995b. Straw: the next great building material? The Last Straw 11:7.

_____. 1996. Insulation comes of age. Fine Homebuilding 3/96:46-53.

Wilson, A., and **J. Morrill.** 1996. Consumer guide to home energy savings. American Council for an Energy-Efficient Economy, Washington, D.C. and Berkeley, CA. 267 p.

Wolfe, R. 1993. Low-cost pole building construction. Garden Way Publishing, Charlotte, VT. 178 p.

Wright, F. L. 1954. The natural house. Horizon Press, New York, NY. 223 p.

Wylde, M., A. Baron-Robbins, and **S. Clark.** 1993. Building for a lifetime: the design and construction of fully accessible homes. The Taunton Press, Newtown, CT. 295 p.

Hybrid design with straw-bale walls carrying half the weight of each shed roof.

Photo by Matts Myhrman

Photo by Matts Myhrman

Out On Bale workshop participants raising eight-course-high structural walls, using three-string bales layed flat.

Index